Self-Regulation

A Family Systems Approach for Children with Autism, Learning Disabilities, ADHD and Sensory Disorders

RONDALYN WHITNEY, PHD, OTR/L
WENDY PICKREN, MS, OTR/L

PESI
Publishing
& Media
www.pesipublishing.com

Copyright © 2014 by Rondalyn Whitney, PhD, OTR/L and Wendy Pickren, MS, OTR/L

Published by
PESI Publishing & Media
PESI, Inc
3839 White Ave
Eau Claire, WI 54703

Editing: Bookmasters
Layout: Bookmasters
Cover Design: Matt Pabich

Printed in the United States of America

ISBN: 978-1-937661-30-4

PESI
Publishing
& Media
www.pesipublishing.com

Open the Doors to the Village

Newly constructed houses become a village once a place for the residents to come and celebrate spirit is added to the center of the community. Whether this epicenter is a church, a lush park or a meeting house for quiet reflection, the place where spirit dwells, grows and is honored distinguishes a town or hamlet from a cozy village. *And . . .*

"It takes a village to raise a child." - African proverb

Real quotes from real people in our village:

H.P.
"What I want to do and what my brain tells me to do doesn't always match."

C.C.
"As a teacher, I want all of my students to be successful. But, I don't even know where to start."

Z.A.
"I have been told that 'You get what you get, and you don't make a fit'. But, I really DO wish that I had parents with more experience."

M.O.M.
"I need to see my son make real progress in his real life. I don't want to be my son's frontal lobes all of his life."

A.A.
"Everyone picks their nose. Cool kids are good at hiding it, but us weird kids aren't."

O.T.
"I want to really help the families I work with, but I find that the goals I set don't always end up addressing the real problem that the child is having."

Table of Contents

Rondalyn's Acknowledgments

I am the mother of two amazing boys, who swell my heart, grey my hair, and remind me how much effort it takes to make parenting look like the kids grew through their self-authored, intelligent design. Thank God for my rock and partner, their dad and my husband, Bill. He is our Christopher Robin.

I was raised in a village, the small town of Milton, West Virginia, where I was loved and my writer's spirit nurtured. My own mother, Maggie, taught me with her words and actions that a mother's job is to make memories that will warm their child across a lifetime. I am grateful for her example. My mother-in-law, Linda, has been a champion of family, and she provided me with a strong example of the role of mother that I can only hope to embody.

Nothing of value, in my opinion, emerges in isolation. Scholars like Jean Ayres, Rosanne Shaft, Winifred Dunn, Paula Kramer, and Lucy Jane Miller have constructed a body of knowledge that this book used as its foundation. I'm blessed to work with brilliant colleagues; Varleisha Gibbs and I have collaborated on our Self-Regulation presentations for audiences throughout the United States. Some of the ideas in this book were inspired by her amazing insights.

I thank the team at PESI, and my editor Linda in particular, for the opportunity to share this story with you. Finally, I acknowledge my co-author, Wendy, for her Village Approach for WISER Interventions and the precious gift of her friendship.

Wendy's Acknowledgments

Whether I refer to my own family-system, my best friend (and sister) who literally lives next door, the children and families I work with from whom I learn more every day, my circle of friends who are continually working together to build lives that work well and feel good, or our larger community, I understand that it really does take a village to raise a child. I appreciate the playfulness, compassion, and mutual determination to support each other in reaching our goals that feel "just-right" and even those that can feel much too challenging at times.

To the many mentors I have had in my professional career and Linda Jackson at PESI, I thank you for holding my hand and whispering, "Grow..." To Rondalyn, my dear friend and colleague, I love you for not being afraid to ride the rollercoasters with a smile on your face and your hands held high. Your love for life and learning is contagious, and I am thankful to have you and your magic in my life. To the LAW Society and Amy Washburn, my partner at THE VILLAGE and my friend for life, thank you for meeting me at the station, jumping on the train, and smiling with your eyes as we head through this wild ride together.

To my husband and my own children, thank you for your daily reminders that life is precious. To my mother, I owe you a debt of gratitude. You inspire me with your grace and boundless enthusiasm. I have had the opportunity to grow empowered in your sunlight. You remind me to ask myself, as is asked by the poet, Mary Oliver, "What will you do with your one wild and precious life?" My answer is, "The challenge is ours for the taking, and I plan to open the doors and accept it."

Preface

More and more, we realize families need interprofessional care if they are to create optimal outcomes in the lives of their children. This book will use an interprofessional approach to encourage therapists to think holistically, use theory to guide their intervention, and focus on a Family Systems model to create optimal outcomes. This book follows the most up-to-date evidence related to optimal outcomes for children and youth and their families. We have imagined this book much like building a house, starting with pouring the foundation, framing the house, and finishing the walls. Once the process of moving into the home and becoming connected with the greater village has begun, we have observed the emergence of new sets of challenges to be considered and addressed. In our final section, we offer techniques for assessing and intervening regarding these challenges, and give multiple case studies to bring theory into practice for families, teachers, and clinicians.

In the first section, we build the foundation by outlining some of the meaning behind living with a differently developing child. We open doors and invite you into our homes, share stories we have collected during our years as therapists, and tell you our own stories. What we have learned from the amazing families we have had the opportunity to work with could fill many books, but we have chosen some specific examples that may hit close to home for you. In this section we will think about what we really mean when we say "it takes a village" and outline some of the occupational roles, performance patterns, and contexts that ultimately build the capacity for families to generate health and well-being in the face of life's inevitable stressors. Here we build our conceptual model for the book, translating the evidence for supporting optimal outcomes related to overall family quality of life. Beginning in Part I and continuing throughout, we provide cases to expand the concepts, present evidence-based rationale for "what families want," discuss the gaps often left exposed within current practices, and offer recommendations on how to build a variety of bridges to close the gaps. Models of health-related quality of life, occupation as both treatment and a practice, and why "it takes a village" are concepts we feel are essential to understand if we are to truly couple and promote the potential of children and their families. The importance of habits, routines, and role clarification as unifying constructs are introduced in this section.

We have imagined the second part of the book much like framing a house, translating theory into practice. Part II will open the door to information, theories, and frameworks that are used to guide interventions and ultimately structure problem solving. We will use case studies to deepen understanding because that is how we learned; by co-creating solutions with our clients and their families over the years. Children's actions and habits are largely based on what they learn from their senses. When sensation is perceived in a faulty manner, faulty behavioral responses are predictable, such as sensory defensiveness or poor modulation resulting in poor self regulation. This section explains how the sensorimotor system works, defines sensory processing (sensory integration in a nutshell), and outlines how disorders of sensory processing can negatively affect learning and social participation. Here we connect the dots between theories, guiding readers in the selection of relevant theory for the case.

Neurobiology is complicated. When explained well, parents and teachers can use their understanding to decode child behaviors and provide strategies that promote sensational learning. In this section, we provide a rationale for how integration of the senses is needed for learning, as well as intervention strategies for each sense. Case studies are included in the chapter to guide you through the ideas we present, as if we were all consulting around the table within our therapy clinic. Whitney's model of "Sensory Pooh" is included in this section. The authors conceptualize a "toolkit" being built for the reader to guide the accumulation of tools for sensory-sensitive learning.

In Part III, we finish the house by providing management tools for you to use during intervention. Whether you are a therapist or a parent stepping into the role of interventionist, this section is designed to give you hands-on strategies to tackle the major known barriers to achieving family quality of life. We hope to guide you through critical reasoning and problem solving, empowering you to better assess and provide support for sensory-based disorders impacting learning and social participation. Using Whitney's problem solving strategy, which we will refer to as the WISER Approach to Treatment Planning and Ongoing Assessment, we will guide you through the essential process of identifying the root of the underlying problem, providing you with strategies to balance the scales of sensation and beginning to understand the strengths and challenges of each sensory profile. The importance of play is covered, including features that promote or inhibit play, how to playfully enfold sensation into day-to-day life, and the importance of creating an integrated system (sensational), to promote positive mental health. Methods for distinguishing sensory dysfunction from maladaptive behavior will be included.

In our appendix, you will be guided to reflect on the different aspects of the book and use worksheets to guide reflection, much like we use in clinical practice. We think of this section as the time to move in and enjoy the neighborhood and to begin to acknowledge the important role that integration into the larger village plays in successful participation in a child's occupation. To that end, we focus on what will empower parents, clinicians, and teachers to synthesize principles for a sensory-sensitive life and to open the door to social participation for families raising a child with a disability. This section includes activities and problem-solving strategies as the primary teaching method.

In our minds, no book on intervention would be complete without a good set of appendices; We highlight available evidence for the importance of sensory-sensitive parenting and teaching as essential ingredients to support optimal learning and empowering our children to be socially savvy. Sensory-sensitive tools are found everywhere, and we've provided some ideas about how you can use everyday activities to promote optimal participation. Our appendices will help guide you in your quest to build your own toolkits from available resources found in most kitchens, recycling bins, and other hidden treasure troves in the environment.

Each of this book's two authors has multiple roles: mother, occupational therapist, friend, coach, writer, entrepreneur, educator, daughter, sister and wife. But it takes a village to write a book or, perhaps, to create anything of worth, and behind these two authors are sons, psychologists, families, clients, speech pathologists, and more. We hope to speak with a village voice and in so doing, create a path for the readers of this book to open their own doors and step forward into a sensational life within thriving communities. No one is an expert on everything, including us, but together we hope to build a community of practice that celebrates the wonders of childhood, the tools of science, and the power of a committed family to empower children to successfully be active participants in their villages. Open the doors and join us in our quest.

About the Authors

Rondalyn Varney Whitney, PhD, OT/L

Dr. Rondalyn Whitney joined the staff at the University of the Sciences in Philadelphia in 2012 and currently serves as Assistant Professor of the Doctoral Program and research mentor. Dr. Whitney writes prolifically on the barriers to optimal quality of life for families when living with a disability, sensory processing and social participation and is the author of the seminal book *Nonverbal Learning Disorder: Understanding and Coping with NLD and Asperger's - What Parents and Teachers Need to Know*. She is a dynamic and respected national and international presenter, speaking on ASD and related topics, is a content expert on sensory processing, narrative as a therapeutic modality, social skills programs, autism and related disorders, using technology to reduce barriers of access to quality care and quality of life for families raising a child with a disability. Dr. Whitney is one of only 7 OT Champions named by the American Occupational Therapy Association and frequently called upon to serve as a media representative for the association.

Dr. Whitney served at one of the Centers of Excellence, Kennedy Krieger Institute's Center for Autism and Related Disorders as a Senior Research Coordinator (IV). She coordinated the multi-site, 3-year federally-funded study examining the effectiveness of school-based social skill interventions, solving problems with recruitment, intervention protocols and research procedures with outstanding results. She is the lead Investigator of the study *Quality of Life among Families of School-Age Children with an Autism Spectrum Disorder in the United States*, presented at the International Meeting for Autism Researchers and the American Occupational Therapy Association and *Online Journal Writing, Maternal Stress and Mother-Child Relationships Among Mothers of Children with Pediatric Psychopathology*. She is currently in the final stages of development for the prototype of innovative Serious Game in partnership with IsoDynamic.

Dr. Whitney's research interests are in Family Quality of Life, health related quality of life, toxic stress, emotional disclosure through personal narrative, and using innovative games and technology to overcome barriers to optimal care. Her primary outcome variable of interest is enhanced social participation for individuals with disabilities and their families.

Wendy Pickren, MS, OTR/L

Wendy Pickren is a co-founder of **IT TAKES THE VILLAGE** in Northern California. Members of the collaborative interdisciplinary treatment team at It Takes THE VILLAGE provide occupational therapy, psychological counseling, speech therapy, and psychological and educational testing for children and families needing extra help. The continual collaboration between these therapists and the family-systems perspective results in a uniquely comprehensive intervention program which utilizes both traditional and innovative techniques to facilitate the family's ability to create and sustain optimal outcomes.

Ms. Pickren earned her Master of Science in Occupational Therapy and Certification in Early Childhood Special Education from San Jose State University in 1994. She has extensive experience in supporting children and their families in their home, school, and community environments. As the "occupation" of a child typically involves self-care skills, communication, gross and fine motor skills, education, and socialization, she focuses on the foundations of sensory processing and psychosocial and physical development during meaningful activities. Since 1994, Ms. Pickren has emphasized getting to the heart of the matter when supporting children and their families in creating lives that work good and feel good.

PART I

Pouring the Foundation—Theory

"Everyone has a story. If you knew my story . . .
you might change your mind about me."

What story are we telling about our children? Those we work with, those we parent, those we spy having a temper tantrum in the grocery store? What story do you want your students, children, or clients to tell about you? Dr. Robert Brooks often shares the story of a child who came to him because of severe school-avoidance. He asked the boy to draw a picture of his teacher. The drawing was that of a huge, red-faced, angry man with a screaming mouth that was wide enough to devour the small child who was cowering below. It is not the picture we want any child to draw of us. Showing that picture to the teacher was a powerful beginning to the solution for the school-avoidance problem.

Parents can help children solve problems, just as therapists help clients solve problems. Larson suggests we think of this activity as a dance, an orchestration that includes planning, organizing, balancing, anticipating, interpreting, forecasting, perspective shifting, and meaning making. The process of balancing takes into account the desires of individual family members, prioritizing occupations to bring harmony to the family in a way that creates stability within the family. Parents need to make key decisions when setting priorities and synchronizing occupations, and they then must select among competing needs to create a harmonious family environment.

Therapists often become scholars of the role between stress and immunity, anxiety and illness, and the connection between being unavailable to respond to life in a way that balances the little things with the big things and the overall feeling of well-being. Are you a parent? A teacher? Take a minute and think about how you respond when a child spills a glass of milk. Do you scream? Do you focus on the milk and the soaked items in its path? Or do you focus on the child; the one who accidentally reached too far or too fast and created a small disaster? Do you give the message that the child is the treasure or that the milk holds greater value? Do you take time to consider what influences the child's situation? For example, is he stressed because he's being rushed? Was the glass too big for her muscles to control? What is hiding in the background of the child's behavior? What is hiding in the background of your response? Granted, a gallon of organic milk can be priced like a treasure, but at the end of the day, will the liquid be important or will the spirit of your child? Sometimes we have to pause and reflect on what our priorities are.

I saw a note other day taped to a friend's bulletin board that was written in first-grader script: "Thanks for loving me even when I make mistakes." That's the note I want to tape up! Don't you?

No Parent, No Child is Perfect

Being a good parent is not an innate skill, even though some people can make it look that way. We must resist comparing our inner selves with another person's outer self. I remember sitting in an audience once, behind a "perfect" couple—they had three "perfect" children. We were watching our son (who we all knew wasn't "perfect") deliver his kindergarten performance, knowing that just yesterday he had a tantrum so intense he broke the principal's phone. I was jealous of those parents sitting there with their cameras (being "not perfect," we forgot our camera). The next week, however, I got a call from this mom. Her son had been diagnosed with bipolar disorder, autism, and a string of other labels. As it turned out, the imperfections in their life made ours look much closer to the perfection that I had perceived theirs to be. I was flooded with compassion for my overly harsh, self-judged self who had been sitting in that audience.

The interactions between parents and their infants have been described as a dance—a dynamic, reciprocal exchange between the participants—and provide the basis for later motor, gender-role, social, cognitive, and language development. The nature of this parent-child interaction is thought to be a strong predictor of a child's optimal development.

How we play can be different, the roles within parenting can be uniquely constructed. Mothers play with their children; they play with toys, spend time reading with them, and engage in attention-getting activities. In contrast, Nakamura and colleagues found that fathers tended to spend more of their time engaged in play that was more physical: games that included bouncing, lifting, and rough-and-tumble play.

Parents are the conductors of the orchestra: family, chores, school events, spills, stomach flu, bike wrecks, and all that life brings to us.

Activities that are playful and engaging tend to invite greater participation. As a result of the meaningful nature of these activities, children can unknowingly practice important skills. Play researchers Knox, Schaaf, and Burke explain that environments that provide space for movement and exploration promote play and engagement. In contrast, those environments that constrain or confine movement by exposing the child to too many dangers (think of being in the section of the store with lots of fragile glassware) inhibit play. Having options for play, with objects or people that entice children to touch and experience through their senses (touch, smell, taste, listen, move), can promote play. Environments that cause children to feel self-conscious or overwhelmed by novelty will tend to restrict play behaviors. Children want the opportunity to repeat experiences. Hitting the drum over and over or repeatedly singing the same song into a real microphone, a reverberating toy microphone, or even one made of a toilet-paper roll builds mastery. In addition, finding the "just-right challenge" is important for play; too much competition or too great a challenge can impede play and create frustration for your child.

In the clinical practice of occupational therapy, it is important to understand and address the needs of parents as well as the needs of the child being treated. More than 100 years ago, Antoine de Saint Exupéry's *The Little Prince* taught us to understand "What is essential is invisible to the eye." Olson and Esdaile's seminal book on occupations of mothering suggest that even though the role of mother and the activities they engage in may be unseen, these essential efforts form a silent backdrop against which therapeutic efforts on behalf of a particular child are provided. A client and mother of a child with severe sensory dysfunction burst into tears at our clinic as she related the following story, revealing that initiating individual treatment for the child alone would not be sufficient intervention in this family:

> *I'm exhausted. My son won't leave me alone, and if I try to give my attention to my daughter or, God forbid, to myself, Paul will have a meltdown. Yesterday we were at a restaurant. We were hungry and the food was taking forever to arrive. Paul began to scream and kick me. My four-year-old daughter got scared and started to cry and claw at me. We were essentially in a wrestling match in the booth of the restaurant and people began to stare, shooting those daggers of judgment I've become so used to. I asked for the food to be wrapped to go and endured the manager's critical remarks while continuing to wrestle with my now completely out-of-control children. After we finally got to the car and I completed the battle to get them buckled in as they thrashed and screamed, I cried and cried. I am embarrassed to say this, but for a moment, I thought of just leaving them in the car and walking away.*

You never know what is happening behind your neighbor's closed door. Compassion is the antidote to judgment.

One day, my neighbor who had just had her second child approached me in the driveway on her way back from the mailbox. Usually perfectly quaffed, that day she had on shorts and a sweatshirt, her hair swept up in a straggly pony tail. I felt reminiscent of the joy I felt as a new mother and asked how she was enjoying her new life with a new baby. She told me:

> *All in all, we're doing pretty well these days. Today was a particular scream. My mom is visiting and insisting on revamping the garden (which means she needs compost and a driver to take her to get some). My "dream baby" was unwilling to nap, my going-on-two-years-of-unemployment husband was at a job fair, and my four-year-old with a sensory processing disorder put down his beloved dinosaur toy and said "My tummy hurts" before proceeding to throw up in the pile of my new baby's clean laundry! All the*

while, I have not even brushed my teeth today, and I've not showered since Monday. But before I could take a single minute to take care of myself, I cleaned up my son's vomit; tucked him in with a heating pad, tea, and a Dora the Explorer video; began to rewash the baby's now barfy laundry; and surrendered MY kitchen to my mother as she made five dozen rolls for our family (although I am trying to lose the baby weight and am on a no-carb diet)! All I can do is laugh, although all I want to do is cry. I just hope that my laughter will fill my system with endorphins! Heaven knows I could use some.

Interventions should promote and sustain improved quality of life for families in the family system that they really live in. Interventions should use what we know about sensory processing and strategies that help children modulate sensation so they can do their good work (be a good friend, be a successful student, be an active participant in the family). More importantly, we want to translate what we know from the science of therapeutic intervention into the day-to-day lives people live. In so doing, we hope to offer a story of meaning, understanding, and ultimately management of the daily stressors that are indeed inevitable when raising a family. The idea of a "normal" child and a "normal" family only exists in statistically contrived numerical averages and standardized deviations. Parents who partner with a therapist to find meaningful interventions for their child can significantly change the trajectory of that child's development, opening the future to positive possibilities that would otherwise be missed. We see this every day; trust us—a lot of change in development can happen.

How We Make Sense of Our Own Worlds

The stories we tell are our way of explaining what we see; our explanatory model for how we make sense of our world. One's explanatory model is invisible but essential to the way a person experiences his or her world. We believe that children want to be good, and paying careful attention to their actions can teach us what may help them meet this goal. We strongly believe—and more and more the evidence is supporting our clinical intuitions—that interventions can facilitate the most significant improvements in function and satisfaction when those intervention are guided by strong evidence and theory. When working with children, we have developed some interesting protocols about how to approach some of the challenges that we stumble upon in therapy sessions with children; like how and why it is not the best idea to point with your middle finger, how to write on your homework page while never touching the "itchy" part of a pencil or hearing the irritating squeak of the lead across the page, and what to do with a booger when you have pulled it out.

Kids need to know the basics, and we try to answer their questions in the spirit with which they've been asked—with logic and a light-hearted commitment to solving real-world problems with the child. We hope to partner with you and share our understanding that we each, normally, have to problem-solve our way around extraordinary circumstances, puzzling child behaviors, and heart-breaking ignorance that judges us and leaves us feeling small. We can make a world of difference for families who feel lost in the chasm of day-to-day challenges. By helping families understand, find meaning in their occupational pursuits, and learn how to manage the inevitable stresses of life, we can help them open the door to health and well-being. Ultimately, our goal is to improve the quality of life for families raising a child with a significant disability or even a child with a slight difference in development. Together, we can create a village that is welcoming, supportive, and provides a context in which children and their families can thrive. Between us, we bring more than 40 years of collective experience to this project. Perhaps more importantly, though, we bring the stories of those who have found supportive routines and rituals and gifted us with their lived wisdom: the families and children who have allowed us to be a part of their homes, their communities, and their village.

If we can, as a village of committed partners, translate some of our knowledge, journeying behind the doors of intervention for a number of children, and share our thought processes and resolutions, then perhaps we can begin to use the Little Prince's wise edict and harness the essential; that which is hiding in the background but ultimately creating barriers to well-being. For parents, we hope to convince you that no goal or desired therapeutic outcome other than improved quality of life in your family should be enough to have you open your wallet and pay for a session of therapy. We hope you will join our quest to build villages, ones with spirit and understanding, a common sense of determination to find the "just right challenge," and to remind ourselves to "put on our own oxygen mask first." We need to work as a team so we can ultimately love our children when he spills the milk or she wrecks the car, as well as all of the moments in between when our children make mistakes.

THE STORY YOU TELL MATTERS

When a new apple variety or rose emerges in a garden, we celebrate our good fortune— nature has created a new variety, a new lusciousness for our eyes or palate. Do we welcome the differences in children, encourage the uniqueness, and seek to make way for its optimal sweetness? Nature has an either/or message for us: grow or die. Water that does not move is putrid; plants that cannot push up from hardened soil wither and die. Fairies are said to be the tenders of nature, assigned to assure the direction of growth in individual plants. They stand by and whisper silently, "Grow." What does your child hear whispered?

Do you view your child as a disaster zone, always creating chaos? Or is her enthusiasm and curiosity viewed as the breeding ground for the next Nobel Prize winner? Are we promoting and nurturing growth and diversity? Children can be amazing scientists. They want to explore and test the world they live in. Some children are determined researchers; they test the world and those of us who live in it with an unrelenting commitment. Begin to think about how to help your child problem-solve and gather feedback, to look at the data he is generating and use that to form new hypotheses and create new (more adaptive) explanatory models. Encourage them to be researchers, to experience the world, to learn by sensing—feeling and touching and tasting and moving and seeing and hearing. This helps children think about what things are and how they work and to store the information in multiple ways (*how heavy, how soft, how salty, how fast, how bright, how rockin'?*). Each time a child experiments, investigates, explores, and experiences the world through her senses, she builds on her ability to problem-solve, hypothesize, and invent. Because his exploration is interesting and meaningful to him, he develops a longer attention span, the ability to focus, and the likelihood to realize greater competency. Their memories are stored through many, many connections, linked with emotion, making them seekers of a greater sense of wonder. When a child avoids the world around her, she self-deprives, and limits her ability to learn or integrate her learning and is unable, then, to apply discovery to solve the next problem. Children often need our help to make sense of what they are finding; if he feels overly bothered by tilting his head in the bath for a shampoo rinse out, he may come up with the faulty conclusion to his experiment that one must avoid baths all together. You can use the scientific method to become an aggressive researcher just like your child by observing the behavior you see, generating a question about that behavior, forming a hypothesis, and setting about gathering information or data to help you answer your question. Children teach us about their research questions, their hypotheses, their data, and their conclusions. It's our job to help critique and shape their scientific method.

But Miss Wendy, I like to eat my boogers—they're salty. My friends say I'm gross, and my mom gets mad at me, but I like it. What am I supposed to do?
Gabe, I have lots of other food that is salty and warm. Let's try some of those instead.

How do you understand this story? What meaning do you find in the child's story-telling to the therapist? We have to pause and disclose some of our fundamental beliefs. Children want to be good, to participate in their world, to learn and grow and be part of their social fabric. When that isn't happening, we need to identify for the child those characteristics that prevent optimal engagement and contribute to learning inefficiencies, irritability, and family impairment. When a child with a developmental delay in the sensorimotor is paired with an adult who is inflexible or has created a story about the child's behavior as something that will benefit from compliance to the adult's will, we can predict with high probability a less than optimal outcome. However, when a child-adult relationship is one with a good fit, the adult has the capacity for compassion and recognition of faulty processing hiding in the background of the child's poorly chosen strategies. In this case, we can predict a more satisfying outcome, one of collaborative problem solving and instruction. The adult might say, "I've noticed that bathtime seems especially irritating for you." Supporting the child as she sorts through the responses she has at her disposal, being open to feedback, and selecting the one that will produce the most positive result will ultimately bridge the gap between the developmental delay and optimal growth. The key is, perhaps, being open to feedback. The adult must create a relationship of mutual respect and offer solutions that fit with the problem in order to build trust with the child as a collaborative problem solver. Although invisible to the eye, this *therapeutic alliance* is essential. A child's actions and habits are largely based on what they learn from their senses. Piaget, as well as other developmental theorists, pointed out that sensory information provides an important foundation for learning and behavior. We learn through the senses. All nerves to the brain are sensory nerves, bringing in information about how things look, feel, taste, smell, and sound. They bring in data on how heavy something is, or in what direction we are moving in relation to the environment. We then have to immediately and unconsciously organize what we take in; Have we seen this color before? Have we tasted this flavor before? Do we organize it with something we like or do not like? With this carefully categorized information, a reaction in direct response to our perception of sensation occurs. Knowing this process, we can observe behavior and know something about an individual's sensory perception. We can learn about sensory perception and processing and make good predictions about potential behavioral responses.

Kramer and Hinojosa's formative text outlines the theoretical framing of the function–dysfunction continuum when approaching treatment. When faulty sensory perception goes in, faulty motor responses come out of the nervous system. Dysfunction in sensory processing is a developmental delay, and deficits in the sensorimotor system can compromise a child's capacity to respond to adult directions without non-engaging behaviors. For example, when a child is overly focused on her internal sensations (tags irritating her, noise perceived as painful, a very distracting runny nose), she is not available to attend to external demands (looking at peers to recognize social cues or hearing the teacher's instructions). You may see a child crawl under the table and refuse to complete his math assignment when he is attempting to get away from the scratch-scratch sound of the pencils used by his tablemates.

FAULTY SENSORY PROCESSING = FAULTY RESPONSE (VIEWED AS DISRUPTIVE BEHAVIOR)

Understanding the problem may give adults better capacity to employ strategies that will net positive results. We all have some inaccurate perceptions of sensations, but the extent to which we have automatically or conscientiously employed compensatory strategies predicts our success in social relationships, work, and activities of daily living. Actions based on faulty processing of sensory input can result in faulty responses, which are often viewed as disruptive behaviors. Yet, if we can identify the sensory patterns or faulty false alarms (he brushed up against me and hurt me), we can begin to predict the less than optimal results (kicking, screaming, biting, hitting) of that faulty perception. The goal is to reduce the frequency, intensity, and duration of maladaptive strategies for coping with underlying sensory processing dysfunction. Socially disruptive behaviors can impair progress in academic skills, impede achievement of developmental milestones, and create impairment in family routines, social participation, and quality of life.

When incompatibility occurs between a child and the environment, we may see outbursts or withdrawal. When demands exceed a child's capacity to respond adaptively, we must seek to make sense out of what the child's behavior is telling us. As adults, it is our role to take the child's perspective, to identify what barriers are in the child's way, and then to partner with that child to remove those barriers. Partnering with a child can improve her ability to participate in the occupations of a child: play, school, and being a cherished member of a family and a community.

We tell stories about children: *This child is the bad kid. That child can't behave. The child over there is a terror.* The stories we each tell are filtered to our own experiences, our expectations, and our internalized ideas. But as the adult, we actually get to recraft our own story and in so doing, the story of our children.

A psychologist once told a mom, "Your son is a bad child and you should tell him so." The mother tells this story years later with new anger and says, "I left that day and never took my son back to see that awful man. I held my son and told him he was good and I loved him every day after that. He is a fantastic young man; everyone agrees. Shame on that psychologist! He couldn't see my son's sweet spirit. Imagine if we had taken on his story about our child!"

We tell stories about children every day and they in turn create stories about themselves:

- Imagine your child comes home and says, "William's dad says I'm a bad boy." Allow yourself to just pause and sit with that message, let it sink in and experience that lack of social censure delivered from a father to a child and through that child to your child and now to you as the parent.

- Imagine your child comes home and says, "Mrs. Seik threw an imaginary drop of kindness today toward me but it landed like a boulder, making me feel warm and happy all over." Allow yourself to just pause and sit with that message, let it sink in and experience that social story delivered from a teacher to your child and to you.

- Imagine coming home from the hospital after visiting your sister who is fighting breast cancer, and seeing that a teacher has sent you an email saying, "I met with your son today to help him get caught up with his trumpet. Wow, he is a great kid."

- Conversely, imagine coming home from the hospital after visiting your sister who is fighting breast cancer, and seeing that a teacher has sent you an email saying, "Your daughter has to practice more. She was an embarrassment to herself today!"

- Imagine your child asking, "Mommy, am I a bad boy?"

- Imagine your child saying, "Dad, do you love me no matter what?"

We tell children stories . . . and children repeat those stories as fact.

In our work, we say, "You are a sweet child with a kind spirit, but sometimes your behavior and your words don't match your inner sweetness, and other people can't see your true self. We need to work together to develop better habits of using kind words and actions so you are a match inside and outside." We believe that children often are who you tell them they are, and become the adults you told them they would be. When we whisper to them, "You can grow this way . . . I have confidence that you can grow that way" . . . they may listen to us and grow in the direction of our story about them.

ARE EXPECTATIONS REALISTIC?

Stories are built around our internal working models related to a child's capacity for conformity and adult expectations for obedience. This story of a strong willed or disobedient child sets up embattlement. We would like to present a new story, a peaceful warrior story. These children need our help to be their wonderful selves. We are at war only if we choose that position. We would like to invite you to join us as problem solvers instead, and create a story of childhood as a place where children can shine because the adults understand the just-right challenge for them, and create well-suited opportunities for growth and development. We envision a story of families who flourish because their expectations of their children (and themselves) are realistic. We invite you to consider that the issue is not problem children; instead, it is a misfit between expectations and capacity to respond. If that is truly the case, the goal is to piece together the sensory puzzle so we can make learning and living sensational for children and their families.

The story you tell brings meaning to your life. When a family learns their child has a difference, something inside them may shatter. Anyone who has heard "your child has autism" or "ADHD" or "cerebral palsy" or any disability has lived through a "death" of the child they had imagined they would have. One world falls away, and the family has to create a new life— one that may look much the same to the outside world but to the inner family everything, and nothing, is different. Some families have grieved and taken action to accept the reality of the children in their lives, and some have not. As therapists, we have to offer help with this process. Some families are in "denial," but in our experience, denial is merely a placeholder until the family finds meaningful and solid footing instead of a shattered illusion.

Salutogenesis is the outcome we want to achieve: the ability to generate a new meaning, manage resources, and understand our situation. Families are hoping we know how to help them achieve this new place, a place of wellness and wholeness. Some families figure out how to reach this place on their own, and some need a bridge. The term *salutogenesis* is the ability to create or generate health and well-being even in the face of life's inevitable stressors. Occupation—activity that is meaningful and purposeful—is used both as a treatment in our practice as well as a positive outcome of treatment. For exaample, we can use the occupation of cutting with scissors as a way to develop the outcome of participating in the family's routine of wrapping gifts for the annual Cub Scout Christmas fundraiser at the mall. Our roles (of parent, teacher, child, student, sibling), our routines, and our rituals are performance patterns that we use to engage in our daily occupations.

Opening doors to full participation and salutogenesis takes a village.

Areas of occupation related to taking care of your body, or activities of daily living (ADL), include bathing and showering, bowel and bladder management, dressing, personal grooming and hygiene, sexual activity, toilet hygiene, eating, feeding, functional mobility, and personal device care.

SNOT Protocol

Explaining to a Kid What a Booger Is and What to Do About One

Occupational therapists are health care practitioners who have received training to provide intervention for the occupations in your life, including areas of occupations related to taking care of your body.

These ADLs constitute actions within our day-to-day lives. Although most children learn the social rules of many ADLs, many of our children need to learn these rules in a more overt, direct way. We often need to articulate or narrate the mundane to make it obvious. Some children need help to control the muscles of the mouth so they can spit. Spitting is a critical skill for oral hygiene, eating, and swallowing. But by far, one of the most common complaints from adults is children who pick and eat their own boogers.

Children have an innate drive to seek meaningful experiences from their environment even if the adults don't like how they've chosen to do so…

The SNOT protocol was developed to help children learn the social rules for the occupation of caring for the naral region of the body. Taking a sensory approach, the nostrils, or *nares*, are interesting holes in your head. They are highly innervated and hyper-responsive to the smallest amount of debris lodged on the skin or dangling on one of the many hairs that serve as protectors against infection. The nose is an erogenous zone, although perhaps you haven't conceptualized it in that way. The nares lead straight to the brain and channel sensation of smell immediately to the sensory nerve for olfaction. Olfaction is the only sense that does not pass first through a relay station in the brain, so you can think of it as a nonstop flight. Conversely, the sensory pathways involving vision, touch, hearing, proprioception, vestibular, and taste all have layovers at various airports in the head.

Olfaction is primitive, and tactile input in this region is, by neuroanatomical design, quite alerting (or bothersome). When dirt or dust gets in our noses, it get stuck in nose hairs, and the mucus or snot surrounds it, traps it, and makes it into a tiny trash package ready for removal. Those "cornflake" projectiles in the nostril feel like boulders and not specks, getting our attention, and we are highly incentivized to remove them.

Talking about boogers is not "polite talk," and children are often left to their own resources to figure out this system. Even though the nose does have mucus instead of snot, there is no medically euphemized or socially appropriate word for *booger*. A booger is a booger. And kids love to hear an adult say that. Like, instead of *snot*, we say "mucus," but if it's a booger, it's a booger.

Grossology (fun science about yucky stuff in your body) is an area of great interest for most kids. Mucus is important and is found all over nature, coating your skin and hair and all your organs. Boogers are dried-up snot or trapped material you have inhaled such as dust, pollen, sand, fungi, smoke, and germs. Mucus traps those potential invaders and keeps them from getting into your lungs.

Because the body has worked hard to trap and remove the dirt, you too want to get it out. If you remove it with your finger, you have that dirt on your hand and then it is transferred to anything you touch. If you eat it, you're eating that dirt or germ so your body went to all that trouble to take out the trash and you brought it back inside. (Yuck!). If you wipe those germs on your sister, then that is gross too. This is why grown-ups nag you to put it into a tissue and toss the tissue with the snotty booger into the trash. You've helped your body get rid of a problem and haven't made your booger someone else's problem!

How many other words for Boogers can you come up with?

loogie
ball of snot
cornflake

_____
_____
_____
_____
_____
_____
_____
_____
_____
_____
_____
_____

What are ways that you can deal with a Booger that are okay for your health and don't gross other people out?

_____
_____
_____
_____
_____
_____
_____
_____
_____
_____
_____
_____

The original SNOT protocol appeared in *SI Focus* magazine.

PART II

Framing the House—Incorporating Theory Into Interventions

Remember the African proverb,
"A child does not grow up only in a single home."

Dr. A. Jean Ayres was a visionary scientist whose research led her to theorize what is now known as the *Sensory Integration Theory*. Dr. Ayres's work explained what she observed to be patterns of developmental delays in children with learning inefficiencies and deduced the association between sensory input and behavior. Dr. Ayres's theory is grounded in developmental principles and neurological postulates. Sensory integration is considered a developmental process. As a neuroscientist and an occupational therapist, Dr. Ayres used her theory to explain her observations and design interventions guided by principles of neurobiology to resolve fundamental deficits that impact the occupations of the child (the occupations of learning, play, and being a family member). Postulates or fundamental core assumptions of the theory begin by stating adequate processing and integration of sensory information and are an important foundation for adaptive behavior. The work of occupational therapists has evolved to include Sensory Integration Theory assessment and treatment using the Ayres Sensory Integration Approach (OT-SI). Some practitioners have begun to use the term Sensory

Processing Disorder (SPD) although this is not an established diagnosis. Still, SPD is being used with increasing frequency.

And, it is important to note that all individuals process sensation in our own, unique way, so a diagnosis of Sensory Processing Disorder would only be pertinent when such difficulties impair day-to-day routines or roles. When sensation is perceived in a faulty manner, predictable faulty behavioral responses might include sensory defensiveness or poor modulation, and this will result in poor self-regulation, emotional volatility, and maladaptation across environments. The story we tell is our way of explaining what we see, it is our *explanatory model* for how we make sense of our world. Individuals' explanatory models are invisible but essential to the way they experience their world. If we have an explanatory model of a threatening sensation, we will react with fear and anxiety. Maladaptive emotional regulation can look like hitting, kicking, lying, acting "weird," and biting, while adaptive regulation looks more like asking for a do-over, matching our face to our feelings, or using a sensory strategy to get unstuck and move forward with a new plan. Sometimes emotional regulation can take the form of self-stimulation, which, depending on the circumstances, can be either adaptive or maladaptive. We would consider publicly picking one's nose or self-stimulation of the genitals maladaptive (but in private these behaviors would not necessarily be considered maladaptive).

THE SENSORY INTEGRATIVE PROCESS

Theory guides practice and provides a mechanism from which to frame observations and strategically guide interventions. In the foundational text *Frames of Reference for Pediatric Occupational Therapy*, Schaaf, Schoen, Smith, Roley, Lane, Koomar, and May-Benson worked together to outline 10 postulates of Ayres's sensory integration theory with which to help guide the practice. The postulates align with The Village Framework and support the premise that children have an innate drive to seek meaningful experiences from their environment, and that development of sensorimotor fluency follows a developmental arc. The postulates can be summarized and applied to our purpose.

The first postulate states an optimal state of arousal is a prerequisite for adaptive responses to occur. If an individual has a heightened emotional response to an event in the environment or is in a pervasively heightened state of arousal, that person will likely respond to the events in the environment in a way that may be viewed as overresponsive. In other words, the person is likely to show a lack of resilience when asked to respond to environmental encounters in a developmentally appropriate range of emotion or attention. However, even though this response will be consistent with the child's perception of the environmental precipitant, it may seem maladaptive to other observers in the environment.

Next, sensory integration occurs during adaptive responses. The more opportunities a child has to learn to respond in adaptive ways, the greater the development within that system and subsequently to progress toward integration within the nervous system. Third, multiple sensory systems may be needed to facilitate an optimal state of arousal. Think about hearing someone scratch fingernail across a chalkboard: your immediate response is to employ a second sensory pathway to help you organize that sensation. We can predict, from neurology, what choices you may make. You might scream or jump up and leave the room in an attempt to avoid the sensation. This is both a limbic and a motor response. You might grit your teeth or provide pressure to your ears; each a sensory compensation response. Other examples include chewing gum, chewing on your pencil, or drinking something hot such as coffee to help you feel organized when you are nervous.

The fourth postulate suggests that adaptive responses must be directed toward a child's current developmental level. Similarly, the fifth postulate states activities that reflect a *just-right challenge* and occur within what Vygotsky coined as the *Zone of Proximal Development*. The just-right challenge provides a milieu for sensory integration to occur. And the just-right challenge is interrelated with conditions in the environment that serve as deterrents or encouragers of development.

It is important to balance developmental readiness and safety.

Let's take, for example, the developmental skills necessary to open a door by turning a doorknob. Fundamental abilities include gross grasp, wrist stabilization, forearm rotation, activation of large muscle groups, and momentum. Meanwhile, the use of chopsticks or a carrot peeler would require more advanced abilities, which also include skilled prehension and finger dissociation.

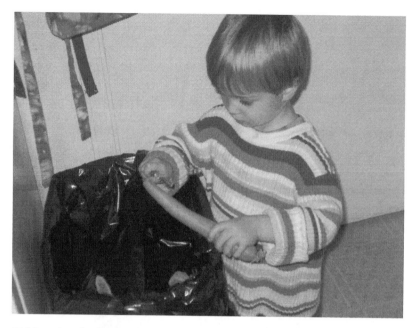

Children develop fine motor skills and habits of helpfulness when they help the family prepare meals. Working together to cook dinner is a routine that supports family quality of life.

Being familiar with the developmental progression of skills, one would reasonably assume that a child would learn to open a door before being able to use chopsticks or a peeler. However, you could also imagine a child raised in an apartment building with a door that opens to a flight of stairs would be *deterred* from learning to open that door, while Asian parents might *encourage* the use chopsticks or a family that values everyone helping with tasks related to meal prep *encouraging* the use of a carrot peeler. Thus, a child might present with an atypical developmental pathway, precocious in one area and delayed in another. This type of environmentally-induced sequence of skill development underscores how development occurs interrelated to societal expectations, interpersonal engagement, and the dynamics of doing.

Problems with sensory modulation or foundational abilities contribute to deficits in end-product abilities. This sixth postulate provides an alternative explanatory working model for tantrums, avoidance, or delays due to ecological factors. Imagine a child who avoids dressing activities because she finds the change of temperature (related to taking clothing on and off) overly alerting to her nervous system. The child has a meltdown (maladaptive response) each time she is challenged to dress independently. Mom provides easy-to-don/doff clothing (no buttons, zippers, or snaps) and helps the child each day. This compensation provides an additional burden on the family and deters development for the child. The *just-right challenge* then might be to provide warmed clothing or partner dressing with tight hugs or rubbing to reduce the perceived threat of overstimulation of the tactile nervous system. Adding chores to the child's daily routine may help to expose her gradually to sensation, allowing her to habituate over time. Moreover, it helps build adaptive habits, and distributes the work so the family has more time for leisure and the house is tidy and restful.

One-Minute Chores

Make a list of chores each person in your family can accomplish in under 2 minutes. For example:

Mom's Monday Chore: Wipe out the bathroom sink with a Clorox wipe.

Dad's Monday Chore: Replace all the towels in the bathroom.

Zac's Monday Chore: Wipe off the bathroom mirror with a Windex Wipe.

Alex's Monday Chore: Put all the towels into the hamper.

The next and seventh postulate suggests that, when a delay has occurred in the development of sensorimotor skills, a child needs to be self-directed, with the guidance of a skilled therapist, for sensory integration to occur. Relatedly, the eighth postulate expresses the concept that adaptive responses are elicited through activities that facilitate sensory modulation, discrimination, and integration, resulting in improved postural control, praxis, bilateral integration, and participation. When parents, teachers, and other adults provide children a sensory-rich learning environment and support their participation within that environment, children's nervous systems can grow and develop. When internal delays result in avoidance or other disorganized interactions with the environment, and the adults are knowledgeable about the way the developmental delays in the nervous system can impact adaptive responses, the adult–child relationship predicts increasingly adaptive responses. Conversely, when the adult responds with insensitivity, the irritable child becomes anxious and responds with less than optimal strategies, a spiral predicts exacerbation of the developmental lag rather than remediation and adaptation.

A child's performance in school, with friends and with their family routines, can be most successful when the demands of the task, their developmental skills, and the environment are congruent. Challenges that are too great can lead to negative outcomes.

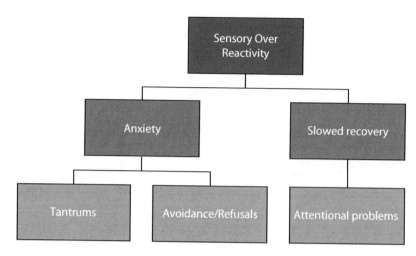

Learning, the acquisition of knowledge, skills, and occupations, is acquired through experience. Because the brain can grow new cells and connections (a concept known as neuroplasticity), enriched experiences effect change in the nervous system. This dynamic process leads to a permanent change in the nervous system and can be seen in a child's behavior and performance. The final two postulates outline how sensory processing and behavior develop concurrently. The research suggests that, when intervention is directed to underlying deficits in sensory modulation, discrimination, integration and/or foundational abilities, and not toward training in specific skills or behaviors, an on-ramp to adaptation is built. The tenth postulate suggests that, as a child achieves increasingly complex adaptive responses in treatment, changes will be evident in outcome abilities such as self-regulation, self-esteem, social participation, academic performance, and participation in activities of daily living. Sensory integration is a foundation for physical and social engagement and participation in daily life activities and routines.

Sensory 101: The Basics: How the Sensorimotor System Works

In a nutshell, sensory integration is an individual's ability to respond adaptively to sensation over a broad range of intensity and duration. When sensory processing is "integrated," the result is an *adaptive response* in which the individual can use sensory information to support optimal arousal, attention, and activity level to meet the demands of the environment in a fluid, flexible manner. Disordered sensory processing can be conceptualized as falling into three subtypes: SOR (Sensory Overresponsivity), SUR (Sensory Underresponsivity), and SS (Sensory Seeking) Kinnealey, Koenigh, and Smith (2011) have shown that elevated scores of modulation disorders (sensory overresponsivity, underresponsivity, or sensory seeking/craving) have been shown to be heightened predictors of internalizing (anxiety, depression), externalizing (behavioral outbursts, kicking, hitting, fighting), and dysregulation problems (heightened emotional responses). The results of these underlying problems are often impaired family quality of life, decreased success with academic skills, and impairment in socialization skills. Difficulties in sensory modulation are often the first signs that parents notice in children with ASD. By-products of a developmental delay in the sensorimotor area can result in atypical sensory processing. These children may present as poor sleepers, poor eaters, difficult to soothe, and unresponsive to others. Children may unconsciously use less-than-optimal strategies in an attempt to regulate their arousal state. These strategies may include hand flapping, rocking, or head banging in their more extreme forms, or fidgeting, avoidance of eye-contact, and humming in their more mild forms.

When we process sensation in a productive or adaptive manner, our neurological system is said to support optimal arousal, attention, and activity level in such a way that we can now meet the demands of the environment. Struggles in one's ability to process, make sense of, and adaptively respond to sensation are often referred to as disorders of sensory processing or, at times, a sensory processing disorder. Current disagreement about confirming the diagnostic term *Sensory Processing Disorder* has not stopped this term from being used to describe difficulties with sensory processing that get in the way of a child's ability to play and learn and be a good friend.

Think about how we have to first register information in the sensory system, or, to be more technical, the receptors have to fire in response to a stimulus. We then process the input and finally organize it for use, creating adaptive responses within the environment. Within this framework. Instead, atypical responses and actions are not the child's willful attempts to make life chaotic, instead the child's nervous system is unconsciously reacting to sensation.

Lives in the Balance . . .

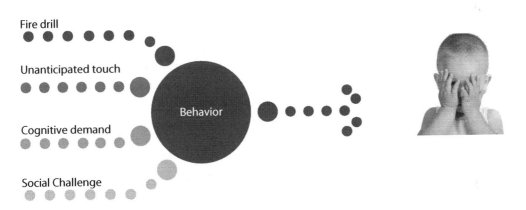

The nervous system is an organized system; all nerves to the brain are sensory nerves and all nerves from the brain are motor nerves. You can observe an individual's motor response and make a pretty sound guess about how that person's sensory system is taking in information. For example, have you ever seen someone at an outdoor picnic leap up, yell, and wave hands and arms frantically around his head? When you see this, you can guess he "felt" a bug crawling on him or "heard" a bee buzzing around him. Sensory in, motor out. This scene is funny when you know the person is overreacting to a plastic bug: He has faulty information coming into his nervous system and so his motor response is "faulty" as well. Sometimes it is funny to watch, but if you are that person and you are really afraid of bugs or bees, it's not so funny.

The opposite end of the loop works too. You can know someone is really sensitive to noise and that if you turn the TV on and whoever watched it last had it turned really loud, the noise-sensitive person will, most likely, jump or complain or hold her ears. If you understand the way an individual processes sensory information, you can often predict how that person's motor system will react.

Ayres's Sensory Integrative Approach takes advantage of these theoretical constructs to develop interventions. If you say, "Mom, I need to turn the TV on, and Granddad was watching last so it's going to be loud for just a minute until I can turn it down," then Mom is prepared and doesn't have to startle or defend against the noxious input to her nervous system when the television loudly blares to life. Similarly, many children can benefit from the warning about an impending sound that has the likelihood of creating a fight-fright reaction, such as "Head's UP! I'm turning on the BLENDER!"

All learning occurs through the senses because all nerves carrying information to the brain are sensory nerves. We learn through our eyes, our ears, our noses, our taste buds, our hands, our muscles, and our system of detecting how our head is moving. We also have receptor cells that give us information from inside our bodies. These interoceptive cells are in our organs and tell us in a crude way how we feel inside (e.g., Are we hungry?). The interoceptive cells in our stomach tell us this information. This system also gives us information about heart rate, digestion, state of arousal, and mood.

We demonstrate what we have learned by expressing that information to our motor system. We might raise our hand to indicate that we have heard a question; we might smile when we see someone else smile; we might write a note after we learn a new vocabulary word. Sensory in, motor out. Faulty in, faulty out. Children's actions and habits are based on what they have learned from their senses. If they have learned that every time they get out of the tub their skin prickles and hurts, they will anticipate that unpleasant (or painful) sensation and work to avoid experiencing it. If they do perceive this reaction to be painful, they will go out of their way to avoid the sensation. We might say they are defending against it. In fact, we might call it sensory-defensive behavior if we see it often. As a protective response, children can be quite aggressive in defending their state of well-being.

Other children might not even notice sensation. They might have a cut with blood dripping, but be unaware of it and unable to tell you how it happened. These children have what we refer to as an underresponsive system. And still others might have trouble regulating or modulating sensation in which they don't necessarily feel avoidant but once the sensation gets into their system, they don't know what to do with it. You may have experienced this phenomenon when you got on a ride at an amusement park. Everything seemed okay at first, but all of a sudden you realize you are going too fast or are being thrown too hard against the side of the cart. Maybe the "spook house" is too scary, but you are stuck for the moment and you have to hold yourself together until the ride is over. Because children don't know when the "ride" is over in much of life (a trip to the mall, music class, etc.), they sometimes respond to that state of not-knowing with the fight or flight reaction in the form of a tantrum instead.

Difficulties in sensory modulation are often the first signs that parents notice in children with ASD (Baker et al., 2008). We can take for granted all the sensations a nervous system must take in and process, even in a simple task. Imagine this situation: your child is playing at the Children's Museum in the waterworks area. Think about the sensation in this environment. What is available to his visual system? Olfactory? Tactile? Auditory? Proprioceptive? Vestibular? We ask a lot of an immature nervous system, even when we provide a sensory-rich opportunity for learning and play.

Now, imagine this child being deprived of all this rich learning because when he does go to the museum, he gets overwhelmed and "acts out."

Like turning on water from the faucet to fill a pitcher, you can have too little, too much, or just the right amount fill up your pitcher. Too much and you will have overflow, splashing, and often a mess. Too little and you will need to take more time to get enough. Sometimes you might have intermittent water pressure. In that situation, you are waiting for the trickle and then SWOOSH, you get overwhelmed by the unexpected gush. You might even get startled or angry by this gush and throw the pitcher, breaking it, as you attempt to get away from the onslaught. Sensation can be thought of as a way of "filling up your pitcher" in your own nervous system. We might see the last "drop" and think that is what caused the behavioral response when, really, it's the accumulation that causes the spill over.

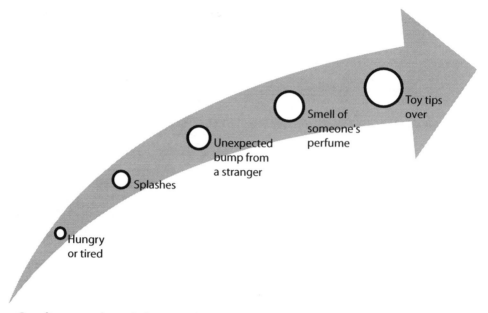

Our lives are about balancing this information as it comes into our nervous system. Researchers Ahn, Miller, Milberger, and McIntosh estimate 5–15 percent of children, within the general population, show signs of sensory modulation difficulties that affect their social participation, academic success, activities of daily living, and family quality of life. Many researchers suggest a much higher prevalence of atypical sensory processing is found in clinical populations, for example, autism and ADHD. For example, Tomchek and Dunn's research suggests in addition to core features of ASD, 95 percent of children with ASD also present with atypical sensory processing. Sensory overresponsivity and ADHD are estimated to co-occur in 69 percent of individuals with ADHD. Perhaps it won't surprise you to learn that researchers (Green & Ben-Sasson, 2010; Pfeiffer, Kinnealey, Reed, & Herzbert, 2005; Lane, Reynolds & Thacker, 2010; Baker et al., 2008) find a strong relationship between sensory sensitivity/avoidance and anxiety, as well as between hyporesponsiveness and depression. Approximately 25 percent of children with ADHD also have anxiety disorders.

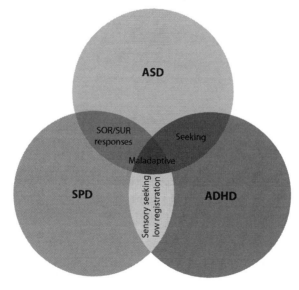

Dr. Miller and colleagues identified three key sensory integrative abilities, each with secondary subtypes:

Type I. Sensory modulation

Type II. Sensory discrimination

Type III. Sensorimotor skills

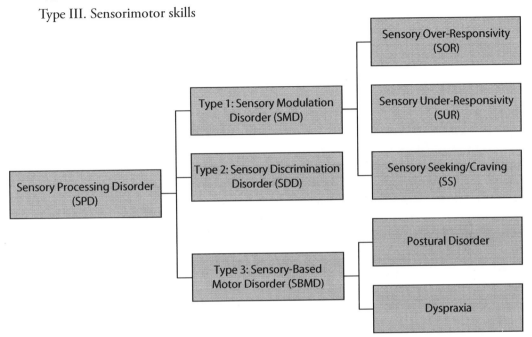

Conceptual Framework for SPD
Adapted from Miller, et al, 2007

Like all developmental milestones, a child's developmental level related to each of these key areas can range across a continuum. Kramer and Hinojosa present this way of organizing our thoughts about development and disability as a function–dysfunction continuum. We can think of function–dysfunction continuums overall as the range of ability to integrate or modulate sensation.

SENSORY MODULATION MODEL

SPD Type I: Sensory Modulation

Winnie Dunn has developed a strong body of knowledge related to sensory processing and modulation. Modulation means to adjust or adapt, to regulate one's response to the expectations in the internal or external environment. Miller suggests three primary subtypes of sensory modulation: *sensory overresponsivity (SOR), sensory underresponsivity (SUR),* and *sensory seeking/craving (SS).* We modulate our thirst when we feel the internal sensation of thirst and get a drink. We modulate our alertness when we shift our position, sitting up straight, to focus on the speaker. We can think of modulation with the voice or a musical instrument; the musician varies the pitch, intensity, or tone of the voice or instrument in order to create an overall harmonic. **Modulation is ultimately a derivation of the word *measure*; we measure our responses and when successful, we would be self-regulating.**

Poor modulation or poor modulation occurs when the individual's ability to respond adaptively to sensation over a broad range of intensity and duration is in some way impaired. Using Kramer's function–dysfunction continuum, the concept map might look like this:

Ability to modulate sensation for
adaptive response

Able to modulate in some environments

Able to modulate in the morning only

Able to modulate with one sensation but not
multiple sensations at once

Unable to ability to modulate
sensation for adaptive response

Sensory modulation within Ayres's Sensory Integrative Approach can be conceptualized as an individual's ability to respond adaptively to sensation over a broad range of intensity and duration. When we are successful in self-regulation, we can achieve and maintain optimal arousal, attention, and activity level to meet the demands of the environment. Our ability to modulate can be altered by experience as the nervous system adjusts and grows in a process called *plasticity*. Modulation includes both physiological and behavioral responses. **The unobservable piece, modulation, is the physiological response occurring internally within our central nervous system, while the observed response is *regulation*.**

Sensory Overresponsivity and Anxiety

Sensory overresponsivity (SOR) has been described by Dunn and others as a condition under the broader umbrella of a sensory processing disorder (SPD) that presents as a state of dysregulation (irritability, poor modulation, hyper - or hypo-responding to sensory input) and low habituation (lack of successful adjustment to sensations in the environment). When we struggle to adapt to our environment, or are overly vigilant, we feel anxious. Often this anxiety causes behavioral responses. For example, a child who is overly anxious about the feel of a toothbrush in her mouth might have a tantrum in the attempt to avoid that sensation. This can also be viewed as the "fight" option in the fight-flight response pattern.

Overresponsivity refers to having too much information entering our sensory systems, which in turn creates high arousal levels. Your child then needs to attempt to slow down the amount or rate of incoming information. A behavioral response is then elicited. If your child has a low threshold for sensory stimuli, he may overreact. Crying or screaming behaviors may be his attempt to block out the unwanted stimuli. Sensory overresponsivity (SOR) is being reported at high rates in children with and without primary diagnosis such as attention deficit hyperactivity disorder (ADHD) and autism spectrum disorders (ASD). Winnie-the-Pooh can be conceptualized as a sensory overresponding character. He tries to limit sensation by only wearing one color (red) and limiting his activities and food groups. Although most people think of ADHD as "high arousal," the nervous system is really experiencing low arousal: The child is actively seeking ways to re-alert himself. We need to look for healthy or unhealthy ways children have discovered to "balance the scales" and offer them optimal, adaptive strategies.

Sometimes, SOR is severe and we consider that level of sensitivity *sensory defensiveness*. When a child is defensive against sensation, we have to understand that her perception of the sensory information connects with the sympathetic nervous system and triggers the fight, flight, or freeze response. The F/F/F response is an adaptive response that keeps us away from danger by helping us avoid noxious input. Under the influence of sensory defensiveness, however, a person's system reacts to non-noxious input as if it were noxious. You can see a defensive response because the nervous system sends a message to the muscles to tense, the pupils to dilate, and the heart to beat faster (to get away from that threat!). The stimulus may actually hurt the individual even though you may find that same input underwhelming. The F/F/F response also collaborates with the limbic system, helping you learn what to be fearful of and what to avoid. The limbic system holds onto those memories related to sensory stimuli and even when the sensation is not present, just the *anticipation* of the input can trigger a sympathetic nervous system response. Even when we learn to tolerate the input, even long after habituation occurs, we may still be influenced by "learned behavior" and react when the sensation is presented to us. Think of how you might react to a snake, even if it turns out to be a plastic snake Or think of Owl in the Winnie-the-Pooh stories. Owl, who really would prefer you to NEVER bother him, has learned that any input is an annoyance.

Sensory Underresponsivity (SUR) and Sensory Seeking (SS)

On the other hand, sensory underresponsivity (SUR) can occur when too little stimulation is being registered. Think of underresponsivity as having a high threshold for sensory stimuli. The gateway needs a lot of sensation before realizing any input is coming into the system. When an individual is underresponsive to sensation, he may seem tuned out (a passive way of responding) or he may seek out input in an attempt to feel alert (active responding).

According to Dunn, passive strategies are observed in kids who seem checked out, tuned out, or underwhelmed by life. They are usually lethargic, slow to respond, and hard to get excited. Think of Eeyore as a passive underresponder to sensation. Seeking behaviors can present as frequently running, climbing, crashing, and jumping (gross motor strategies), chewing on one's shirt or pencil tops (oral motor strategies), or smelling items in an excessive way. These behaviors are active strategies. These individuals share similarities with Tigger in the classic Winnie-the-Pooh tales. Tigger is a seeker of sensation!

See the next few pages for a 10-step countdown to see if the kids in your life are Tigger, Pooh, Eeyore, Owl or Rabbit.

How to know you are a Tigger

10. If you have been told to "stop fidgeting" or "tapping" today
9. If you like to try new routes and shortcuts to everywhere
8. If you move your furniture around, often just "for fun"
7. If you have 10 or more unfinished craft projects that you're "in the middle of"
6. If your desk is decorated with lots of taped-up stuff
5. If you've ever won an eating contest
4. If you have only two speeds, 100 mph and off
3. If you have knocked over your glass so frequently your family has changed the Thanksgiving tablecloth to plastic
2. If you're the FIRST to jump up and play rough and tumble games with the kids at an adult event

and the number one way to tell you're a Tigger . . .

If you've ever yelled "doggie pile!," painted your face purple for a Raven's game, or had a bucket of ice poured over your head by friends

Tigger types are the seekers and speakers. They need us to provide them with some room to bounce, kick, wiggle, squirm, talk it out, and run it out, and we need to feed their need for sensation!

Balance the Scales

- Take frequent wiggle breaks.
- Intensify foods with spices and texture.
- Shake it up! Take new routes! Move the furniture!
- Listen to music, chew gum, and have fidget toys on your desk.
- Add bubbles to the bath.
- Blow on whistles.

A child with sensory seeking/sensory craving (we'll call this child a *Tigger*, with an ounce too much bounce!) needs more sensory input than others to feel in sync. They actively find sensation in their environment, and not always in a way you would choose for them.

How to know if you are a Pooh

10. If you've ruined more than three articles of clothing by cutting out the tag
9. If you have worn the same shirt/outfit multiple days in a row when you think you can get by with it (and it's comfy)
8. If you shop with your hands (based on texture), or with your nose (based on scent)
7. If you own multiple versions of the same shirt (blue, red, . . .)
6. If you are snuggly, but picky about how you like to be snuggled
5. If you hold your nose when driving behind a diesel car
4. If you can identify perfume by name in an elevator
3. If you have moved because the person next to you smells or is too loud eating popcorn
2. If you describe your favorite food by *texture*

and the number one way to tell if you're a Pooh . . .

1. You have gotten up in the middle of the night to search your sheets because you can't sleep and, after finding a grain of sand, fall peacefully back to sweet dreams

"Pooh types are easily bothered." To balance the scales, we need to help them eliminate the extraneous and make their life predictable. They tend to like deep pressure and not tickly touch.

Balance the Scales

- Shop at boutiques and online, not malls.
- Be happy with one color on our plate or a small assortment of tried and true foods (Example: honey [bread is a stretch]).
- Know your limits, use routines to organize.
- Only change one thing at a time and give time to adapt.
- Buy more than one item of a favorite article of clothing; buy in multiple colors.

For a child with sensory sensitivity or avoidant behaviors (we'll call this child a *Pooh*), sensation can feel overwhelming well before it seems that way to others. A mere grain of salt on the fingers can feel like a thorn pricking them or a toxic irritant.

   Such children are often quite reactive and may engage in extreme behaviors in an attempt to get back in sync once sensation has stimulated their nervous system. And because sensation is cumulative, a little bit added to a little bit can feel like an avalanche to this child's sensory system!

How to know if you are an Eeyore

10. If you have turned in an assignment with stains on it
9. If you dress out of a laundry basket
8. If you bump your toe more than once a week
7. If you are used to finding cuts/bruises/ burns and you can't remember how they happened
6. If you commonly have people "groom" you (wipe food off your face, rebutton your shirt)
5. If you have only one speed and cannot be hurried
4. If you have ever had someone "come out from nowhere" and scare you, as they approached you
3. If a bowl of cereal takes you 30 minutes to eat
2. If you can see your belly button when standing up straight

and the number one way to tell if you're an Eeyore . . .

1. You were glad when McDonald's FINALLY added "Warning: Contents of this cup may be extremely hot" to their cups

Eeyores need us to turn things up a bit, but slowly.

Balance the Scales

- Help them "feel" the world first and be alert to their environment. They may need more time and space than you think. Remember, the gateway needs a lot of sensation before realizing any input is coming into the system. They may grow overwhelmed by the time they register that they have gotten enough.
- Eliminate scatter rugs; install guard rails.
- Don't give really hot drinks/food.
- Strengthen resilience (but get their attention first).
- Add one challenge at a time and make sure they master it before moving on.
- Help them build their muscles.
- Be kind—they bump their toes a lot and spill a lot (Eeyores get yelled at even when they do their best).

A child with sensory underresponsivity (we'll call this child an *Eeyore*) will also need to find sensation in the environment to feel in sync. However, unlike Tigger, Dunn's work has helped us to understand that this child is passive and does not seek the needed sensation in the environment. As a result, sensory underresponsive children are often understimulated.

How to know if you are an Owl or Rabbit

10. If you haven't changed brands of soap/shampoo/shaving cream unless it was discontinued
9. If you are mistaken for a hermit
8. If you only drink from one mug, and it's cracked
7. If you love your friends but hope they never ring your doorbell
6. If you have received a gift, saying "Bah Humbug" more than once
5. If your hair is over your face, hiding your eyes
4. If you say the soles of your shoes need "just a bit of repair from a good cobbler" and then they fall off
3. If you wonder why anyone would EVER want something new or shiny
2. If you think car dealers should sell "old car smell" spray

and the number one way to tell if you're an Owl or a Rabbit . . .

1. You are not reading this book new but instead ask a friend to drop a copy when they're all done. You don't want the smell of a new book in your home
- Owls and Rabbits need to know you will honor their need for self-protection!

Balance the Scales

- Use checklists; follow routines and schedules.
- Avoid surprises—help others understand it is an act of caring to prep you well ahead of time for any change.
- Learn what sensory input feels safe; find a brand, scent, or strategy and stick to it (and advocate for yourself).
- Set up your space to reduce sensory input (simplicity and order are your friends).
- *Consider this:* maybe they are not uncooperative, but instead TERRIFIED.

Owls are observers, they can be 'wise' because while others are involved, Owls are taking in data. You can think of an Owl as a person who has sensory over-registration that is so intense, they've learned to avoid sensation whenever possible. Owls, or avoiders, are hyper-vigilant as they try to limit the amount of sensation that comes into their environments. If you are friends with Owl, you are in a small intimate circle of special people.

The Importance of Taking the Time to Take a Good Look

When working with teachers and parents, we explain that we need to think of ourselves as detectives. Detectives need to be observant and look at evidence without judgment. We need to look at a child and observe that child's "actions" as just that, not as internally motivated, emotionally planned "behaviors," but observed actions. Then we can ask what the action is telling us about the needs of the child.

Let's take a pause and consider the children in the following picture. Look at the standing child. What can you say about this child? Limit your comments to the facts, those observations that we would all agree on. When we limit ourselves to describing only the action (and not making assumptions) we can better assess a situation. For example, while the child is smiling (an observation) we cannot assert that he is happy (that is a judgment). Make your list of your observations.

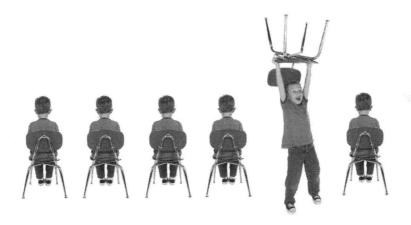

Observations
1. He is standing.
2. He is moving.
3. He is holding a chair over his head.
4. He is smiling.
5. He has one foot behind him, slightly lifted.

We cannot say he is turned away from the teacher; he may in fact be the only one turning toward the teacher. We cannot say he isn't listening; he may in fact be the only child listening. Observing behavior allows us to consider many theories and propose many potential solutions. He is standing, but why is he standing? If we assume he is standing when he is supposed to be sitting, we need to understand what his body needs and if that need influenced him to lift his chair and stand rather than to lower his bottom and sit. Can we provide the sensation to his system so that he can stand AND pay attention to the activity in the room? Learn to be an observer first from a neutral perspective, and think about the hypotheses you can consider. Then, set out with your plan to research your idea in a scientific manner.

When we judge something, or when we refer to actions as "behaviors," the implications are emotionally loaded (e.g., "He is misbehaving," "He is a bad kid," "He won't _____").

Children come up with amazing ideas, and we often have to collaborate with them to make those ideas both therapeutic and socially appropriate.

Think about this situation. Zeke was diagnosed with NLD and even though he was doing well in school in most situations, at recess he was playing alone and "zoning out." His mother and teacher asked the occupational therapist to help Zeke play with others at recess. When the OT observed Zeke, she isolated what she knew (Zeke played alone at recess) and what she needed to know (What need does this separation from his peers seem to fulfill for Zeke?). She reported her findings back to the mother and the teacher. "Zeke is working hard in class. He's focused, on task, and getting his school work completed. He works well in groups and is liked by his peers. At recess, he seems happy, and after recess he is more centered and able to return to class with a good attitude. I think he's using that solitary time to de-stress, to just have some alone time and regroup." The team reflected on the solution and agreed the best intervention for Zeke was to do nothing.

We need to isolate what we know and what we need to know. Sometimes we discover that no problem needs to be solved; and the solution may be, as in this case, to actually change the expectation of the adults in the child's life.

We must all be detectives first, with our skills of listening and observation providing the most important information. First, ask, *"What is this child doing?"* Then later think about why the child is acting in a particular way. Use the worksheets here to practice.

Journal	
Use the scientific method and become an aggressive researcher for your child.	
What I observe . . . (no judgments here; must pass the stranger test)	
My hypothesis (hunger, fear/anxiety, sensory, cognitive, other)	
Method to test out your hypothesis	
Data	
My working theory and future directions	

SPD Type II: Sensory Discrimination

To discriminate is to judge the distinct attributes between two or more objects. Discrimination difficulties are seen when an individual misinterprets sensory information. Maybe the child doesn't recognize the difference between hot water and warm water or between various fabrics. Problems with discrimination can occur in any sensory pathway: visual, vestibular, proprioceptive, auditory, tactile, gustatory (taste), or olfactory (smell). What if, for example, a child can't discriminate olfactory input? Then they would be in danger when others smell smoke and are alerted to evacuate their dorm room while the non-discriminating child stays put. Or if there is a discriminatory problem within the gustatory (taste) sensory system, then perhaps the teen might eat nuts that others in the family quickly would realize had turned rancid. Proprioception is a common area of poor discrimination and causes pencil lead to break (not being able to discriminate force and direction when writing) or disruptions in social success as a result of a child having thrown a ball too hard at a friend. Visual discrimination challenges may result in difficulty distinguishing common shapes or trouble finding items in a drawer or in the refrigerator. The most common way this challenge presents itself in school is in sloppy handwriting or social problems on the playground. When sensory information is imperfect or inaccurately received, performance will be affected as a result.

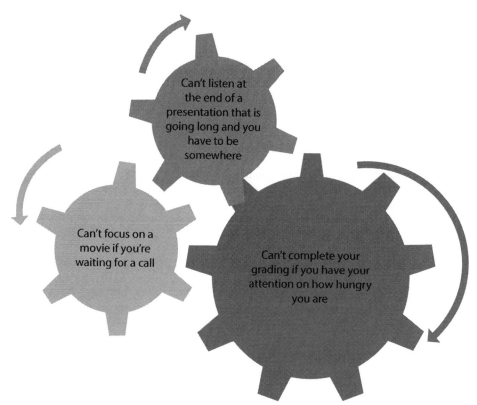

If you are overly attentive to internal sensations, you cannot distinguish the sensory input coming toward you from your environment. Discrimination allows us to interpret and differentiate between the spatial and temporal aspects of sensory information: Where is that sound? What is that taste? When did that smell occur? Discrimination in the proprioceptive system tells us about our body's position or the load on our muscles, and this in turn helps us to adjust the force and direction with which we move those muscles (like when we throw a ball just right to hit the target and dunk the principal in the dunking booth!). Discrimination in the tactile system helps us recognize when we've been touched and how hard we've been touched.

SPD Type III: Sensory-Based Motor System

Parents are more familiar with delays in the sensory-based motor system, indicated by children who are clumsy or don't seem to have enough energy to sit up in a chair, crawl, or walk. Two types of treatable delays identified in the sensorimotor system fall under either postural deficits or dyspraxia. Posture refers to the system that maintains balance and allows you to be alert, resisting gravity. With the popularity of Pilates, more of us understand the importance of core stability. The muscles of the stomach and back work together to hold our entire body perpendicular to the earth. Developmental lags in this system can be particularly challenging for parents to identify, and delays that are subtle are sometimes overlooked.

We listen for complaints that the child is accident-prone, doesn't pay attention, and spills because of her "unwillingness" to be careful. A child can appear strong and even play on sports teams, but when the child is asked to stand or sit still, he sways or fidgets because he doesn't have that inner core stability necessary for extended control in the postural system. We observe whether a child is overly tense in the extremities (like locking the knees) in order to support his or her body. We look for children who enjoy movement activities (running, soccer, football) but when it comes time for sitting still and paying attention in music class, performance is impaired. Sometimes teachers will suspect ADHD, but before moving to that diagnosis—a diagnosis of cognition—the motor system should be evaluated first. Think of it this way, when a person moves, each muscle group takes turns and moves in synergistic patterns. Getting a differential diagnosis will help parents select targeted and likely more effective interventions.

Praxis

Praxis isn't one of the senses, but when we talk about sensorimotor processes, we have to talk about praxis. You have likely heard of dyspraxia or praxis, but you are just as likely to have heard praxis and motor planning used as synonyms; they're not. Praxis is a three-step process in the sensorimotor strip of the brain. It includes having an idea (referred to as ideation), motor planning (making a plan with your muscles to enact your plan), and execution of the plan (the doing part of the process). We measure praxis only with novel or new activities. Novelty provides clues about how to help remediate dyspraxia.

Dyspraxia is overcome with practice; practice makes perfect and perfect practice makes permanent. Riding a bike is practice to overcome the dyspraxia of poor use of the two sides of the body. Climbing up the ladder to go down the slide remediates the dyspraxia of bilateral, reciprocal movements with the lower body (feet/legs). Years ago, children used their bodies to climb trees, jump rope, swing and pump their legs to go higher and higher, tumble down hills, play marbles, play jacks, hopscotch, and so many other activities. These children were receiving large doses of practice in that motor system and had a greater opportunity to overcome any underlying deficits in the sensorimotor system. Today, given our sedentary teaching–learning strategies, our concerns for safety that drive indoor play and the abundant entertainment from technology, children are afforded fewer and fewer opportunities to develop motor skills, and underlying weaknesses can exacerbate instead of resolve these difficulties. Their foundation in their "house" or body is ill-crafted to support the higher floors of thinking, behaving, and joining in social opportunities.

When children use less than optimal strategies in an attempt to regulate their state of arousal/alertness, this atypical sensory processing prompts nonadaptive behaviors (i.e., head banging, hand flapping, tantrums). We also see poor sleeping patterns (poor regulation impairs the ability to settle and rest), poor eating habits (sensory overresponsivity can make one overly determined to limit varied sensory input in the mouth), hard to soothe or prolonged recovery after an upsetting encounter (like a scraped knee), or being unresponsive to others' bid for social attention or social interactions in general.

All learning occurs through the senses

Input ===> Learning ===> application

***

Sensory in ===> motor out

***

Faulty input in (distortion in sensory input)

===>

***

faulty motor out (demonstration of learning / work product)

***

Principles of a Sensory Diet

Often, occupational therapists will prescribe a *sensory diet*, a strategic protocol that offers a regular dose of sensation as a way to balance the sensory needs of the individual.

Quality
- Facilitating
- Inhibiting
- Regulatory/modulating

Power or intensity of activities

Timing (frequency and duration)

Proprioception is joint sense information about the movement, location, and force exerted on joints and muscles.

Heavy work is a kind of proprioception that makes muscles work against resistance.

Deep pressure is firm touch that puts pressure on the skin.

Vestibular considerations of linear versus rotary, or rhythmic versus fast, quick changes.

Typically, in a mid- or "optimal" range, performance, learning, and attention are at their peak. Most adults know how to find this sweet spot for themselves and use sensation to return to this state when they find themselves too far off center. This ability provides the foundation of the sensory diet. Most of us use a sensory diet throughout our day, but we might not think of it in that way. You might, for example, crave or seek sensation around 3 p.m. each day and find something crunchy, something hot, or something especially cold to help maintain your optimal performance throughout the remainder of the day. Or, you might take a walk or stretch, all of which would be helpful to alert your system. You are likely to be specific and habitual about what you select. One of the principles of a sensory diet is the quality of the input (i.e., crunchy, salty, smooth, hot, cold, etc.), and another is timing. Our nervous system has a more intense response to sensation when it is self-initiated and self-administered. A sensory diet helps to supports daily routine and includes play or engagement in occupations, activities that are meaningful and purposeful to the individual. We learn strategies that help us to achieve an optimal level of arousal necessary for cognitive activity, motoric activity, and positive affective tone. Alert attention usually increases with intensity, complexity, unexpectedness, novelty, and affective meaning of input to our nervous systems. In contrast, we are calmed or soothed by sensory input that offers constancy, repetition, familiarity, and neutrality. Look at these familiar situations. What would you do to help yourself be successful when you find yourself in these circumstances?

Think about How you Cope with Your Daily Challenges

Overwhelmed by work, you might:
a) Grab some hot coffee
b) Go for a brisk walk outside
c) Put on some upbeat music
d) Take a nap

You have to study for an exam, you might:
a) Grab some gum
b) Stand up and stretch
c) Listen to the TV in the background
d) Hide your books and hope for the best on the exam

You have to finish your math homework, you might:
a) Chew on a pencil
b) Jump up and down on the bed
c) Sing aloud the new Taylor Swift song
d) Crumple the paper and say your dog did it

Which did you pick?
(a) group suggests tactile strategies
(b) movement options
(c) auditory
(d) strategies you might be tempted by but are not very adaptive!

The three primary goals of a sensory diet are:
(1) to improve ability to modulate sensory input (decrease sensory defensiveness) in order to allow participation in daily routines and support social engagement
(2) to improve sensory modulation and discrimination in order to support optimal arousal, self-regulation, and behavioral organization for learning
(3) to improve sensory discrimination in order to enhance body awareness necessary for sense of self in one's environment and for perceived competence, self-esteem, and self-confidence.

We all find ways to meet these goals but a sensory diet, when created mindfully for individual children, can help them learn what best supports their goals (getting school work completed, being a good friend or family member). Although a 7-year-old child might indeed crumple the paper and blame the dog, the adults will (hopefully) have more mature or adaptive options to offer. When creating a sensory diet, we need to consider the age of the individual, the daily routines (morning rituals or afternoon schedules), access to resources (Can you have snack where you are? Can you go for a walk?), interests and motivations (Would a squeeze toy that looked like a pig or a dinosaur be interesting?), involvement of family, friends, and peers, and safety or contraindications (are there allergies to consider?).

The type of input to consider follows the neurobiology of the sensory system. Because deep pressure and proprioceptive input (heavy work) are helpful to alert us or calm us (we say "organizing"), a sensory diet takes advantage of these principles. We might suggest pretzel sticks or beef jerky (heavy work for the mouth) or a walk (heavy work for the body). We can alert the system with any sensation: think of a whiff of peppermint (olfactory), music (auditory), or the taste of salt or pepper like on salted/pepper potato chips (gustatory and heavy work), or visual (watching a betta fish swim around). Ideally, sensory-based activities should be incorporated throughout the day to help maintain optimal attention. Like a dose of any medication or food, our body takes advantage of the input and then uses it up, needing more as the day goes on. We consider the timing, the frequency, the intensity, and the duration of the input as a way of creating the just-right level of sensation we need to maintain our alert state. A sensory diet needs to help us develop consistent routines and positive habits and to prepare us to transition between activities. Although most of the sensory diet strategies are internal, we always consider the environment as a part of the diet as well, thinking about the temperature, the lighting, scents in the room, and so on. These sensations are "hiding in the background," but once considered, they can be identified as supportive or impediments to function and are then available for triage.

Think about the crowd picture within. Would you like to be in these situations? What do you feel? If you had to be in this crowd, would you feel overwhelmed or invigorated? What strategies would you use to maintain your optimal state even though your system is challenged? Assuming you find these pictures overwhelming and not inviting, and assuming you MUST be in this crowd, what would you do to keep from feeling overwhelmed?

Here are some common responses that an adult with good foresight and awareness of his sensory needs might choose:

Response	Strategy
I would have a drink before I go.	This is a form of self-medication, to relax and reduce the anticipation of the stressor.
I would make sure to wear really comfortable clothes, probably sweats.	Comfortable clothes help us feel in control of the tactile system. This person is thinking of the excess touch she will need to regulate.
I would chew gum.	Smart choice—chewing is a way to get some proprioception into the system and helps us regulate.
I would escape into a restaurant and have a coffee.	This is a good escape strategy, staying away from as much touch/bumping as possible gives us some control.
I would take a friend.	A friend can help us feel less anxious. Because we feel like we can count on our friend to help us, we don't feel so vulnerable.
I would go to the bathroom a lot.	This is an avoidance tactic.
I would have a plan so I knew when it would be over.	Having a plan, knowing when the overwhelming situation will end, is helpful. This is a cognitive behavioral strategy.
I would stay to the edges.	Staying away from as much touch/bumping as possible gives us some control.
I would use self-talk.	This cognitive behavioral strategy can help us feel calm by talking ourselves through a situation.

Now let's take those same responses and think about a child's day:

Adult	Child's life
I would have a drink before I go.	What does a child do? Do they devour candy or junk food on the way to class?
I would make sure to wear really comfortable cloths, probably sweats.	How many children do you know who are "rigid" about the texture and type of clothing they wear? Who insist on wearing sweats and hoodies?
I would chew gum.	What can a child chew on while at school? Gum? Their shirt? A pencil?
I would escape into a restaurant and have a coffee.	Where can your children go? Do they frequently get up from their tasks and wander in the classroom?
I would take a friend.	Sometimes children will overly rely on a friend (or on a parent), and when that friend wants space, your child may feel anxious.
I would go to the bathroom a lot.	This is often a child's way of retreating from perceived threats. How much does the child miss in school when they use this strategy?
I would have a plan so I knew when it would be over.	If a child can conceptualize an ending to the overwhelming scenario, it may be easier to tolerate.
I would stay to the edges.	Do you know children who circle the edges of the playground?

Children's actions are largely based on what they learn from their senses. Neurobiology is complicated but when parents and teachers understand, and help the child to understand their internal system, the child and the adults in the child's life can use that understanding to decode behavior and co-create strategies that will promote sensory-sensitive learning and provide opportunities for social participation.

Other Developmental Theories to Consider

No one theory will ever be able to guide all thinking or suggest solutions to all problems. To begin to conceptualize the world of a child struggling with a disability, we should pause briefly to consider a few other relevant theories. Theory helps guide our thinking when we don't know or can't know everything about a situation. Individuals' explanatory model guides what information they collect, what they consider to be the problem, how they interpret and organize it, and ultimately how they conceptualize a solution to the problem. For example, Einstein theorized simultaneity as a relative construct and created the theory of relativity. He showed that, depending upon where you are standing as you observe a phenomena, you will report a reality of time that might be different from the same reality of time reported by another, AND both of you would be correct. That means we cannot know exact truth, only relative truth. Time, then, is relative. Physicists and scientists accepted this theory as the guiding theory for decades. Now, scientists are expanding the theory of quantum physics, and a new theoretical model suggests that particles are entangled, and when they are, knowing about one particle teaches us exactness about the other. These theoretical constructs guide our understanding of how the universe is ordered, help us make evidence based predictions, create experiments to test our assumptions, and in clinical medicine, provide interventions that are theory-based and guided by the evidence. Ultimately, theory helps us to take advantage of what we know and worry less about what we don't know.

Piaget outlined developmental milestones we can typically expect children to pass through. From sensorimotor to concrete stages of development, children learn from their environment and through their senses to form internal working models of how the world functions. Like all developmental theorists, Piaget reminds us to be mindful that the brain is under construction and is subject to critical periods for learning. When we whisper to a child, they believe us in part because of this evolution of their development. We tell them clapping their hands will save Tinker Bell and up until the age of 10, they will clap with a heart full of the unquestioned belief that they can be a part of the resurrection of a poisoned fairy. We tell them to put out cookies and Santa will rest a minute and nibble while putting out new toys. We tell them they are good and they grow toward that story. We tell them they are bad and they grow toward that story. The mind of a child is under construction, so we must be mindful of the foundation we teach them to construct for themselves.

A 5-year-old child will tell you two pennies are obviously more than one dime because two is more than one. By third grade, children's minds develop and they can understand the more abstract concept of a dime being worth 10 pennies. You can't force a 5-year-old to understand this abstraction; you can overteach the concept and they will use rote memory to tell you the answer, but they won't understand the underlying concept.

Vygotsky expands on this theory by pointing out that learning must occur within the zone of proximal development. That is, the information to learn must be within the developmental range for the child to learn it. In occupational therapy, we call this the just-right challenge.

If we consider a systems theory approach, like the one posited by Bronfenbrenner, we learn one must consider the zones of influence, the interconnectivity, and influences acting upon the learner from the near environment (the family) and the extended environment (the community or society at large). Bronfenbrenner discussed the importance of considering the zones of influence, interconnectivity, and presses when looking at a case and/or considering the success and struggles of a child.

The person-environment-occupation (PEO) model in occupational therapy advances the importance of environment and use of occupations/activities as a way to promote development (Law et al., 1996). This model endorses the power of *doing* and suggests meaningful engagement in activity to support health and well-being.

Two other theories of note include Antonovsky's theory of salutogenesis or the theory of generating health and well-being as it creates a sense of cohesion within a family or organization. Researchers at the Beach Center in Kansas have created the Family Quality of Life (FQoL) theory and provided a body of knowledge showing how the family's sense of cohesion supports or impedes child outcomes. FQoL should be well understood as a critical outcome of interest for practitioners of pediatric therapy. Freedman and Whitney have created a family-friendly guide to incorporation FQoL research into day-to-day family routines.

When considering the quality of life within the family, we think about how the child's development affects the family and how the family affects child development. Although too often overlooked, optimal care considers this transactional influence as a way to open the door to optimal outcomes for the child. Take a moment and answer the following questions on page 43, and then talk about your answers with your partner, your therapist, or clergy.

How could you make getting the laundry completed a sensory task? You can toss the socks in the basket, you can give your child a ride through the house on top of the clean laundry, you can sort socks as a fun visual activity, or you can use scented soaps for a sensory addition. How can you make dinner a sensory-sensitive activity? Think about the feeling of making bread, the smell of chopping lemons for the water on the table, the feel of ice in the glasses, the sight of name tags.

I had a friend tell me about her holiday meals. Each year, one of her aunts purchased various candies—two of each kind—and as family members entered the dining room, each received one piece of candy. At each place setting they each found the matching piece, all different and each matched one to one. Family members had to find their candy's mate and take that seat. Simple acts of sensation make life fun—sensationally so. Take every opportunity you can find to enrich your life with sensation in a way that helps you and your family feel more in sync and more able to participate in the social fabric of life.

Examples of Questions for the Transactional Influences Within the Family	
Family Interaction	1. How often do you have meals together as a family?
	2. Can you and your child share ideas or talk about things that really matter? Do your children share time and ideas together?
	3. Do you have a regular family game night, go for walks, or have other social activities you enjoy doing together?
Quality of Parents' Relationship	1. Do you and your partner share enough alone time together? How would you rate the quality of that time together (1 = not satisfied at all, 5 = extremely satisfied)?
	2. Do you feel satisfied with your relationship with your partner?
	3. Can you name three things your partner did yesterday to care for you or your family?
Support for Person with Disability	1. Can you name three people you can ask to help you even if they would have to go out of their way to do so?
	2. Would you say each member of your family participates in at least one club or enjoyable activity (i.e., plays tennis, member of a Boy Scout troop, plays soccer, mom has a girls night out)?
	3. Are you able to manage arranging the family's medical services or other social events without getting overly stressed?
Material Well-Being	1. During the past six months, has anyone in the family changed a job because of problems related to child care?
	2. During the past month, have you had to leave work because the school was unable to manage your child's behavior?
	3. Are you employed at the level you would like to be?
Physical and Emotional Well-Being	*Physical*
	1. Would you say you get at least 20 minutes of exercise two times a week?
	2. Does anyone inside or outside the home smoke?
	3. In general, would you say you get enough sleep?
	Emotional
	4. In general, do you feel the school does not have to contact you about your child's problems?
	5. Can you name three people with whom you can talk about matters that are important to you?
	6. Do you feel loved by you family, immediate or extended?
Parenting	1. Can you read, tell stories, sing songs or otherwise interact with your child daily in satisfying ways?
	2. All things considered, would you say you can cope pretty well with the demands of parenthood?
	3. Does your child spend just as much time alone without supervision as other children his/her age?

Questionnaire created and copyrighted by Rondalyn V. Whitney, PhD, OTR/L.

PART III

Finishing the Walls and Moving into the Neighborhood—Creating Optimal Outcomes for Improved Quality of Living in the Real World

"Regardless of a child's biological parent(s), its upbringing belongs to the community."
-a Swahili proverb

Every day, we encounter parents whose primary goals are to help their children grow into productive, happy adults. It might be described differently by different families, but it always boils down to the truth that what they really want is for their children to do good things and to feel good about it. In the business world, this same idea is often referred to "On the job success and job satisfaction." When working with children, we refer to this concept as "Do Good, Feel Good." Because of the integral role that families play in all development, family participation is essential in The Village Approach. We must empower parents to use what they know about their own child in the context of their own home to fill their family experience with a sense of well-being and to promote their child's ability to "Do good and feel good."

What happens when you open the door to a sensory-sensitive life? As therapists, we must learn about digestion and expulsion, and come to terms with the reality that, indeed, everybody poops. With that reality, we quickly must adapt our interventions to include protocols for everyday activities like this that include thorough wiping, washing, and pulling up pants after toileting that leave the child able to walk away cleaned up, straightened up (wearing your pants up but twisted to the side is very distracting!), and ready to get back to "work." As occupational therapists who aim to improve "job performance and job satisfaction" at school, we love it when we get permission to enthusiastically hurl projectiles across the principal's desk under the guise of improving oral-motor function or eye-hand coordination. We have supported teens and adults who have upper extremity weakness or poor trunk control or the use of only one arm in the delicate process of donning a condom (over bananas as an adjunct practice), and we've even treated clients who needed assistance reducing sensory sensitivity in order to participate in adult consensual intercourse. In fact, while some say Freud's theory is bankrupt, we might argue the sensory system, and those erogenous zones Freud talked about, are intimately interconnected and do indeed drive our seeking and avoiding behaviors in important ways. We must think about these innate drivers when we consider how our children are developing and how we can support their optimal development. Human beings are motivated to seek pleasure and to avoid displeasure—we can use this understanding of choices and behaviors to create powerful interventions.

When he was four, Alex and his dad were looking at a photograph of a gorilla. Alex insisted he saw an elephant in the photo, although his Dad insisted that he saw none. Dad and Alex went back and forth: "There isn't an elephant," "There is an elephant." Finally Dad said, "Alex, show me. Where is the elephant?" Without hesitating, Alex said, "It's hiding in the background."

When working with children and families, we need to be detectives, observing carefully to identify the problem(s) that are "hiding in the background" and insidiously impairing a person's quality of life. When using a problem-solving approach, such as WISER, you can organize your thinking in a strategic way, guiding your ability to be more deductive and procedural in your approach.

The WISER Approach to Problem Solving

W – What is the problem we need to solve?

I – Isolate what you know and what you need to know.

S – Strategy: Give one a try.

E – Evaluate whether your strategy solved the right problem.

R – Reflect on what you now understand.

Source: Inspired by the work of Polya (1957).

In therapy, we design a treatment plan based on the concerns exposed during standardized testing, clinical observations, and/or parent report. We set goals, implement interventions, and hope to solve the problem. Upon reflection, we may realize that we didn't solve the problem we meant to solve. Or, the problem we solved didn't produce the outcome (i.e., change in behavior) we had hoped it would. More work remains to be done.

At that point, new observations and inquiries must be made, new goals established, and a new treatment plan must be set in motion. However, once again, things are not always as they seem. We must continually be looking for the elephant hiding in the room, because when its presence is clear to one member of the family, all people in the home are affected.

Let's take a closer look at the WISER approach.

W – What is the problem? What is the reason for sensory overload?

- Too much noise, too many people, too much to look at, too many people wanting to talk to you.

I – Isolate what you know and what you need to know.

- Does your child have a meltdown in specific situations? What do you do that seems to help your child feel calmer or get his or her body or emotions under control?

S – Strategy.

- Keep a small bag of strategies with you, maybe a special toy, a juice box with a straw, a water bottle with ice cold water; give a deep pressure bear hug, or an iPod with calming music.

E – Evaluate your strategy and whether it worked: Think like a scientist.

R – Reflect on what you now understand.

Ayres Sensory Integrative Approach takes advantage of these theoretical constructs to develop interventions. Here's another example of communicating a disruption: "I'm making a smoothie in the blender, and there will be a loud noise for a bit." A warning prepares the system, and one doesn't need to startle or defend against the noxious input to the nervous system.

When working with families it is important to always keep in mind that you are working with each of the individuals, as well as with the family unit/system. For example, if the family has four members, you are actually dealing with five members of the family; the fifth member being the family dynamic created by the four members. This last member of the family, the family dynamic, is typically the most challenging to deal with, because it has collective power. We aim to help families create a lifestyle that is sensitive to the unique way we each process sensory information.

Think of a holistic intervention plan as a tapestry and individual treatments as the weaving of the threads within the tapestry. Each of the family members has become accustomed to, and dependent upon, the dynamic created by this family system. Regardless of the functionality of this system, the natural tendency is toward homeostasis. The desire to keep this system static can be both conscious and unconscious. We may be aware of certain ways in which we keep our family dynamic the same, but we tend to lack insight into the unconscious ways in which we do so. Often, this lack of insight is because the parents in the family system bring with them attributes (certain threads of the fabric) from each of *their* families of origins into their current family system, their family of creation. Ironically, these threads tend to be the most unconscious, and parents lack insight about them. Therefore, these threads tend to be some of the strongest threads, holding on tightest and being the most challenging to change, even when they are the most damaging and dysfunctional.

If any member of the family system, any thread of the fabric, is challenged, the entire integrity of the fabric is affected. All of the members will respond to this experience, and some will respond more dramatically than others. However, the natural tendency is to attempt to get back to homeostasis. Because the family dynamic has the collective power, this is often where dysfunctional behavior is created, even if it is not logical. The power of the family dynamic can often feel larger than what an individual member of the family can handle. This intense, complex, and interrelated nature of this powerful fabric of a family system is the reason why we often need to see each of the individuals separately, see different combinations of the family members together, and see the family system as a whole.

> Zoe: I had a terrible day. The whole day sucked.
> Wynn: The whole day? Let's think, did anything good happen?
> Zoe: Lunch was okay and recess too.
> Wynn: Let's draw a clock. So lunch and recess, that's an hour right?
> Zoe: Right, so only 23 hours sucked.
> Wynn: Did you have trouble sleeping?
> Zoe: Okay, eight more hours were okay, and I left school at 3 and things with Mom have been okay.
> Wynn: So, it's 5 o'clock now, so that's two more hours that were okay . . .
> Zoe: Hey, you know what? Really, only math sucked today—just one-twenty-fourth of my day. I guess the whole day wasn't so bad after all . . .

THE VILLAGE APPROACH TO PROVIDING INTERVENTIONS THAT IMPROVE QUALITY OF LIFE

When using what we refer to as The Village Approach, a collaborative team of professionals work together with children and their families to create therapeutic interventions that matter. Essential to all interventions is the family and the areas of concern that are most meaningful, or matter the most, to the child and to the family. Important members of the collaborative team must include specialists in the fields of occupational therapy, marriage and family therapy (counselors), speech therapy, educators, and developmental psychologists. Additional team members may include nutritionists, behaviorists, and other health professionals.

We use the WISER Approach to Problem Solving and base our treatment in the elementary skills of listening and looking. Without such an approach, our ability to use what we've learned—to truly leverage our advanced degrees to change lives—is impotent. Collaborating through the use of The Village Approach affords us the potential to create meaningful change in our clients' lives.

Good therapy begins and ends with listening and looking. After the problem is identified, we use our expertise to guide the selection of the "just right" intervention, carefully selecting tools from a vast toolkit.

Each family has a unique experience in parenting a child. However, as therapists, we often see similar trends in different children. One trend we see is a narrow area of specific interest that affects the child's occupation as friend, family member, or student. These special interests are so intense and the play so rigid that the child is virtually unable to interact and communicate about topics other than his or her own specific favorite. If left to persist with only these topics of interest uninterrupted (by pesky parents, peers, or therapists), the child can wax poetic indefinitely (even *ad nauseam*).

CASE STUDIES

Case 1: Tanner, aka Piglet and the Troublesome ADL

Tanner arrived at our clinic after a long day at his new junior high school. He is definitely the Piglet type: a shy boy with high-functioning autism who is often anxious. You can literally see and hear his anxiety—he breathes with short, shallow breaths. Deep down, he is brave and has had to conquer many scary obstacles to become the capable, personable, prepubescent young man that he is today.

His mother (aka Christina Robins) is a pleasant, cheerful, and compassionate woman. She is a navigator—her children look up to her and have learned they can unfailingly count on her to help them conquer fears and leap over obstacles.

On the way to the therapy gym, which we refer to as "The Playground," Tanner took a detour into the bathroom. As social standards dictate, we waited patiently for him to "finish his business." After 10 minutes of waiting, we knocked on the door asked him if he was okay, and if he would please come out. His mother reported that this situation is not unusual; he often visits the restroom and remains for prolonged periods of time. These detours have affected the harmony of his family in their five-person, two-bathroom home. In addition, the frequent and prolonged bathroom breaks during the school day are beginning to impede his academic success.

We asked Tanner why he spends so much time in the bathroom. He answered in his sweet-yet-squeaky voice, "It is nice and quiet in there. I think it is peaceful in there. I actually enjoy it quite a bit. In the bathroom, I can flush my troubles away."

We explained that his mom was getting concerned that he was taking more than his share of time in the bathroom at home when other family members needed it. We also discussed that when he spends a lot of time in the bathroom, he misses a lot of time in his classes. We explained to him that his mother and We felt it is important to find out if he needed to poop or pee, or if he was just escaping to a place that was quiet and private.

Tanner explained, "I usually like to be in the bathroom 10 times a day, and I would estimate that I actually poop, hmmmm . . . I'd say approximately 3 and 3/4 times a day." This overly-specific response made US laugh. It was the most honest yet hilarious thing we had heard all week. We had found myself squared up against a real-life "troublesome ADL."

Clearly, Tanner's needs for actions were impeding his ability to succeed at his occupation of "student." Our initial thinking was that his need for privacy and for a better-timed bowel and bladder program were going to need some sensitive problem solving. Developing more appropriate options to meet his needs for quiet and privacy would make his life work better and, if created correctly, will also feel like better solutions for him too. Ultimately, we wanted to help him improve his ability to function in the two primary environments where he works (school and home). If we could do that, we could help Tanner improve his ability to be successful at his occupational roles of student and family member.

What was the problem for Tanner? What did we know and what did we need to know to help Tanner thrive? It was time to apply The WISER Approach.

W – What you know/what is the presenting problem?

I – Isolate what you know and what you need to know.

S – Strategy: Try something you think will solve the problem.

E – Evaluate whether you solved the problem you set out to solve.

R – Reflect on what you now understand.

W – What is the presenting problem for Tanner?

Tanner was spending a lot of time in the bathroom at home and at school. This wasn't a problem in and of itself; it's actually a clever strategy or action. The problem is that Tanner's lengthy stays were encroaching on his family time and his academic day.

I – Isolate what you know and what you need to know.

- After listening to Tanner's mother express her concerns, we identified that the frequent and lengthy trips to the bathroom were a problem for Tanner's mom and not for Tanner.

  Tanner had found a workable strategy and perceived his time in the bathroom as a reprieve from a busy and anxiety-producing life. However, Tanner's mom was concerned this strategy was negatively impacting Tanner's ability to learn at school and to be a respectful member of the family at home.

- We needed to know what Tanner was doing in the bathroom.

  o Were his lengthy trips to the bathroom due to a medical problem that was affecting his bowel and bladder functions (side effects of medication, anxiety, etc.)?

  o Was he sitting on the toilet and reading (reading is a favorite activity for Tanner)?

  o Was he talking to himself about favorite topics in what he had found to be a private space?

  o Was he "flushing his troubles away" as he suggested?

S – Strategy: Try something you think will solve the problem.

Creative problem solving with Tanner, his mother, and our counselor began in a supportive and collaborative manner. We opted to start with Tanner's explanation, that he used the time in the bathroom to "flush away his troubles," and identified it as a strategy designed to reduce anxiety. Tanner was able to understand that, although he was not concerned by his time spent in the bathroom, the social implications of this choice were related to what peers would think when he was always in the stalls at school and how his family felt when waiting for their turn in the bathroom.

Together, our team established a plan to decrease Tanner's time in the bathroom by half (Goal: 5 times a day). Our goal was that he could substitute more adaptive strategies into his routine that he would find as acceptable alternatives but would still meet his need for a break.

An intervention plan was created that used sensorimotor strategies aimed to diminish his symptoms of anxiety. This plan, developed in collaboration with Tanner and his family, would provide access to a variety of additional sensorimotor strategies at home and school that would be more age appropriate and socially constructed to allow sustained interactions with peers and the activities in his environment. These options included sucking on ice water through a straw throughout the day, chewing strong-flavored gum, blowing his breath out, and taking a quick walk down the hall to the water fountain at school. Tanner worked with our counselor who introduced Cognitive Behavioral Techniques to help Tanner diminish anxiety throughout his day. She helped him create an enriched visualization of his happy place (a special island covered in his favorite foods and inhibited by his favorite animals), where he could "go in his mind" as needed during stressful situations.

One of Tanner's favorite strategies was "press your pause button." We all need to take a moment to pause every now and then. Some of us do this automatically, others need a visual or physical cue to activate their pause button. Tanner learned to put his right hand on his heart and give a gentle bit of pressure to his chest. With his hand in this position, he then inhaled and exhaled deeply. He liked to "take a pause" and take a momentary trip to his "happy place." Once there, Tanner could assess his current state (under- or overaroused, anxious, sad, angry, happy) and make a conscious decision on how to proceed. While paused in this calm-alert "happy place," he was much more able to choose between multiple appropriate strategies rather than just the one less appropriate option (visiting the bathroom), as he previously did.

E – Evaluate whether you successfully solved the problem you set out to solve.

Did we solve the problem for Tanner? Tanner became able to utilize his visualization and sensorimotor strategies to decrease anxiety, and therefore to diminish his perceived need for this action. Tanner increased his awareness of his ability to effect a change in his own life

During a session two weeks later, Tanner's mom arrived and explained she was having a particularly stressful day. Tanner sweetly said, "Mom, I think you should use your pause button." We all had a good laugh. A momentary pause later we were all on a new track, headed in a potentially more positive direction. We were no longer on the merry-go-round of ineffective habits triggering ineffective responses.

R – Reflect on what you now understand.

We all need options, ways to get away or restore ourselves when we're at the end of our inner resources. The quote, "When you're at the end of your rope, tie a knot and hang on," is a reminder that, when tempted to make a spontaneous and ineffective "trigger response" to a stimuli, having a plan (a series of knots) will help us feel more in control and help us develop a range of adaptive strategies.

When asked if we could share Tanner's story in this book, he said, "Sure. That would be very delightful to show other children how they can find their happy place."

Case 2: Thomas, Omar, Justin, and Pooh: Narrow interests Affecting Engagement
THOMAS

Thomas is a 12-year-old boy. The first thing Thomas says when making a new acquaintance is, "My name is Thomas and I love chinchillas." He then launches into a well-rehearsed and often-recited monologue regarding his beloved pet chinchilla, Chico. At first it is interesting, then it is funny, then it is simply perseverative, and at some point, it becomes annoying to most people (classmates especially). Knowing that he has a unusual family history and particularly important and interesting things happen in his home every day makes it is even more surprising that Thomas is unable to relate even one detail about his daily life that it not Chico-centric.

During collaborative therapy sessions, we were surprised to learn that this beloved "family member" is never out of his cage. Thomas never holds him, plays with him, or interacts with him in any way. Through the intricate details Thomas taught us about chinchillas, we discovered that chinchillas are fast and tend to run and hide. They are not snugglers, they are runners. We began to understand that Thomas's narrow focus on chinchillas and overfocus on Chico were keeping Thomas from interacting with others. We decided to focus our intervention on appropriate emotional attachment.

OMAR

Omar is a 10-year-old boy whose parents initiated a psychological evaluation because of Omar's symptoms of intense anxiety and suicidal ideation, which were impacting his ability to participate in a large variety of Activities of Daily Living. Omar was unable to attend public school because of his intense anxiety, and was therefore homeschooled. During Omar's diagnostic sessions with the psychologist, he remained in a fetal position in the corner of the room. He was unresponsive and did not communicate with the psychologist. Then, during his initial session with an OT and a counselor using The Village Approach, Omar entered the clinic and said, "My parents said I was going to have fun here. So, where's the fun?" The enticing nature of an indoor playground, fully equipped with swings, scooter-board ramps, weighted blankets, and a huge pile of pillows helped encourage him to engage in a child's occupation (play). While playing, we were easily able to begin learning about him, using our tools of looking and listening.

Omar's love for corgi dogs knows no bounds. He talks about corgis, he draws pictures of corgis, he writes about corgis. Omar recently shared a report with us that he had written for school. The title was "Why Each Kid Should Have a Puppy," and the opening line was "Puppies: The World's Best Antidepressant."

We noticed Omar refused to wear shoes (only flip-flops year round). He also bites and picks at his hands and feet and is generally "out of sorts." His parents report these behaviors are consistent with how Omar acts at home.

In comparison with Thomas, Omar actually interacts with the object of his affection. He brought his newest corgi (a puppy with a 12-part name) with him during treatments. His intervention included using corgi-related material to establish meaningful activities with the goal of using his special interest topic as a bridge to cross over to other peers' areas of interest.

JUSTIN

Justin is 11 years old. He presents as a bright, articulate, and handsome young man. However, his mother reports that he struggles with frequent episodes of intense anger, with poor emotional and physical control, which have been occurring with great frequency since Justin was 3 years old. This situation reminded us of the importance of listening to the parents, and then reconciling this information with what we see when we meet the child.

When Justin was 8, his mother brought him to a psychiatrist for evaluation. Justin became so agitated at having to attend this appointment that he became violent; thrashing, kicking, biting, and destroying property in the office. The psychiatrist was so concerned that she called the police and had second-grader Justin taken into custody. He had become a danger to himself and a danger to others.

Justin is intensely interested in technology. He researches and reports on all new technological advances on a daily basis. When he has a desire to own a specific piece of technology (e.g., the newest tablet on the market), he can think of nothing else. He is intolerant to waiting. He is indignant if his parents try to make a plan with him to delay gratification and wait for technology. He must have the item NOW and badgers his parents incessantly until they relent. When in a calm state, Justin is able to identify cognitive strategies that could be utilized during difficult situations. However, he is unable to discuss feelings or implement any of these strategies in an angry or agitated state.

Justin has no awareness that many others do not share his intense interest in technology and is unable to diminish his perseverations. This lack of awareness leads to perpetual conflicts at home and at school, which often accelerate to angry outbursts. A diagnosis of oppositional defiant disorder (ODD) is being considered.

Wynn E. DePooh

DePooh talks incessantly about honey, dreams about honey, searches for honey, and often gets "stuck"—literally and figuratively—in honey. He is intolerant of change: he has one shirt he wears (red cotton) even though it has become so small it barely covers his stomach. DePooh presents with anxiety and is frequently bothered by small changes in his routine.

W – What is the presenting problem for these characters?

The primary problem for each of these characters is an intense fixation on a narrow range of interests, limiting their occupational engagement and social participation. The fixation isn't the problem. Many of us have an interest in something that is a bit "intense," but unless and until it restricts our participation, it is not a problem.

I – Isolate what you know and what you need to know.

- We know these individuals find it extremely frustrating when they cannot engage with their special interest.

- We know these individuals act in disruptive ways in order to get their own needs met (engaging with their topic).

We might want to know more about the environment, the sensory issues, the diagnoses and the other factors that might be influencing the boys' rigid adherence to their topics of interest. In what ways do these interests specifically affect occupation?

S – Strategy: Try something you think will solve the problem.

The four characters were enrolled in activity-based social groups led by an OT and an MFT (counselor). Together, we facilitated perspective-taking, learning to ask questions about or show interest in the other childrens' favorite topics, and practicing good friendship behaviors. Starting with their unique interests (sharing them with the others, engaging in activities related to their areas of interest), we explored the possibility of how each child could take one small step to expand his areas of interest in at least one way. To improve tolerance to the challenge, we provided sensory-based strategies to improve emotional self-regulation (e.g., chewing gum, sour worms, a squeeze ball, and frequent movement breaks).

Given that each of these children had displayed disruptive and sometimes violent behavior, it was also important to help the family and the school create a plan for when and if further action needed to be taken to ensure the safety of one of these children or those around him. These strategies were organized and individualized into sensory diets for each child. Pooh's sensory diet included adding honeycomb, tolerating a new red cotton shirt that stretched over his little belly, and inviting a new friend into the Seven Acres Woods (okay, we made up that last bit).

We added a parent discussion and training group to explore the impact of their child's intense focus and how to help them guide their child to be more expansive in his interests. We also correspond with the school staff to encourage socialization in a variety of settings, with a variety of peers, and with topics covering a variety of areas of interest while identifying socially appropriate ways to include the child's special topics into the classroom curriculum and academic projects.

E – Evaluate whether you successfully solved the problem you set out to solve.

Did we solve the problem? We increased awareness of the importance of perspective-taking in social situations in multiple contexts for these students. We improved conversational skills in a wider variety of topics and increased their ability to incorporate their areas of interest into a conversation while attending to feedback and input from others.

R – Reflecting on this case, how do you feel about intense interests?

More researchers are suggesting we may want to look at intense interests as focused areas of expertise. The way you view an interest will guide how you intervene. Take some time to reflect on what you've learned when you work with children who have intense interests. If we take this simple question and expand it with a theoretical framework, our conversation might look like the following case.

Case 3: Rico

Rico is a real-life Christopher Robin. Rico spends a lot of his personal play time in his own fantasy world, creating realities that he is able to contain and control. Rico's favorite thing to still do at the age of 8 years old is to play with his plastic figurines. He has them talk and communicate constantly. He is powerful in these storylines, as are the figures he plays with. They appear to be afraid of NOTHING.

In Rico's real world, he is also fighting off many "bad guys." These bad guys are comprised of the tags on his shirt, the pants that don't feel good, and the pencil that makes a super offensive sound when he writes. Rico's self-image, his desire to be like his peers, his physical capabilities, and his family's values around sports and fitness persuade himself to often overcome these challenges in order to play sports. The uniforms and equipment are uncomfortable, but his motivation to fit into role of "athlete" in his family system is strong and he is typically able to participate.

As Rico develops and explores the world, he works hard to overcome challenges. When he arrives home, he escapes into his world of characters that are also learning about life through their scenarios of battle, strategy, and victory. Every time Rico rejoins the real world after one of these play sessions he appears more calm, more together, and ready to take on the next abrasion the world has to offer.

One particular challenge has proven to be Rico's nemesis . . . *food*. Rico is unable to tolerate the way food feels and tastes in his mouth. He struggles with how food smells when it is served, even if it is only onto the plate of other family members. Much to the chagrin of his health-conscious and determined parents, all of the foods on Rico's "Will Eat" list consist of white flour–based, virtually non-nutritive items. His typical diet consists of plain penne pasta (yes, the shape does matter), a specific brand of mac and cheese, and any salty, crunchy chip or cracker that is nuclear orange. His specific food tolerances produced food jags for Rico.

Because of Rico's extremely limited repertoire of foods, he and his parents decided to initiate therapeutic intervention. Of particular concern to Rico is that he struggles when at school and when he is on playdates. He becomes hungry but isn't always in a home where they shop in the "Rico Aisle" at the grocery store. Without eating, he becomes grouchy and can even develop severe migraine headaches.

With intervention, Rico is improving his ability to tolerate being around other people who are eating foods that do not appeal to him. Rico is learning to look at, touch, and smell a larger variety of foods. He participated in developing a sensory diet and utilizes sensorimotor strategies to help him prepare himself for mealtimes.

Time to get WISER:

W – What is the presenting problem for Rico?

- Rico's repertoire of food items that he will tolerate is severely limited. It is not providing enough nutrition for his life to work well and feel good.
- He is developing secondary issues of poor self-esteem because of his difficulty with this elemental activity of daily living.

I – Isolate what you know and what you need to know.

- A discrepancy remains between Rico's stated goal of increasing the types of food that he will eat and his resistance to interacting with edible items. He is fearful of putting food in his mouth and eating it.

- What needs to change in order for Rico to increase his interactions with food includes a decrease in sensory defensiveness and an increase in motivation due to social inspiration from peers with similar difficulties.

S – Strategy: Try something you think will solve the problem.

- Explore Rico's motivation for expanding his food repertoire.

- Have Rico participate in SOS food school with a same-age peer who is working to improve the amount of food that she will eat. The peer has no difficulty with sensory defensiveness or tolerating a variety of food items, she simply eats very slowly, thereby ingesting diminished quantities with the result of poor health.

- Make mealtime during treatment playful, changing the way food is "interacted with" and exploring the culture of eating. For example, playing "roll the dice, then take a bite," speed eating, truth or dare, and so on.

- Have his family participate in group therapy to develop a plan for supporting Rico's continued progress with eating at home and in the community.

E – Evaluate whether you successfully solved the problem you set out to solve.

- Within a few treatment sessions, Rico was playfully interacting with all food items presented. Although he was still not eating certain foods, he was able to touch, smell, and lick all items that were presented. As the repertoire of foods he could eat increased, he was also able to increase the speed at which he consumed them.

- By following up with home programs, Rico' was able to sustain gains initiated in therapy and expand upon them in his natural environment.

R – Reflect on what you now understand.

After three months of therapy, Rico stated that he did not want to participate anymore. He stated that he had no recollection of why he started coming to therapy and resisted continuing. Because the sensory-defensiveness that may have been a contributing factor to his initial difficulties with eating had been addressed, and because active participation and external motivation to participate was essential for continued progress in the therapeutic sessions, it was decided by Rico's collaborative team (consisting of Rico, Rico's parents, the occupational therapist, and the marriage and family therapist) that clinic-based therapy would be put on hold until Rico was ready to return.

This decision was a difficult one for the parents to accept. However, after support from the family therapist, the parents were able to acknowledge that the "problem" was not a problem for Rico. He was now content with the foods he was eating, he was not demonstrating any signs of malnutrition, and his ability to participate in the culture of eating had significantly improved. He was now joining the family at the table while they ate, he was tolerating the scents of foods being prepared and eaten, and he had developed strategies for eating when not at home with his desired foods (by bringing a snack bag on all playdates).

Case 4: Andrea

If you allow the melancholic temperament to spiral downward, even when it has good reason, this "mood" or temperament can begin to affect the child's functioning. One example was our client, Andrea. This 12-year-old girl lost her sister, who was her best friend and confidant, to a chronic illness. It goes without saying that this loss was going to have a continued strong impact on Andrea.

Her melancholic demeanor over the next two years started to affect every aspect of her life. She showed no interest in playing, no interest in friends, no interest in achieving at school . . . and specific to our differential diagnosis was a child who appeared to be unable to chew food.

She would often tell her mother that she had no interest in food and couldn't decide what she wanted to eat. Depression affected her occupation as she engaged in very little eating and consequently little use of her jaw muscles. Eating became a huge chore. A child who is depressed and unmotivated is not going to do the work it takes to eat food when it hurts and is ultimately minimally satisfying. As Andrea became more and more malnourished, she got more fatigued. She did not have the energy to play like children do. She took naps every day after school. The situation progressed to the point that even making decisions about what to eat required more energy than this depressed child wanted to exert.

The collaboration of The Village Approach (which included collaboration among the child, the family, the occupational therapist, and the marriage and family therapist) allowed the differential diagnosis to be found and for progress to be made quickly.

Collaboration was significant because Andrea had participated in two previous styles of food-focused interventions, with no success. Andrea had also been seen by a grief counselor who felt that she was improving because she appeared to be moving through her grief. However, this assessment was due to the fact that she is verbally articulate and able to talk about her sister. However, at the same time, signficant physical symptoms were going unnoticed.

W – What is the presenting problem for Andrea?

- Andrea presents as severely depressed.
- Andrea struggles daily with minimal intake of food as a result of depression and secondary complications because of this depression.

I – Isolate what you know and what you need to know.

- Was Andrea motivated to allow depression to dissipate or did a "benefit" come from holding on to this depression?
- Was Andrea's difficulty with chewing truly related to poor muscle strength due to diminished use (atrophy), or was her physical ability to effectively and safely manage a reasonable portion at mealtimes sufficient?

S – Strategy: Try something you think will solve the problem.

- Andrea participated in sessions with the Occupational Therapist and the Counselor (MFT) utilizing the The Village Approach with a peer who struggles with tolerating a variety of edible items. Andrea modeled a willingness to try new foods, and her peer modeled the ability to select and consume foods quickly.
- We assessed the role of depression on eating.
- We explored the family system and how it affected Andrea's ability to release herself from the depression.

E – Evaluate whether you successfully solved the problem you set out to solve.

- We were able to identify that her difficulties were not related to sensory defensiveness nor to poor muscle strength and tolerance for chewing and swallowing sufficient amounts of food to meet nutritional needs.
- We found that Andrea was ready to directly assess her depression related to the death of her sister and discuss a plan to lift the clouds with the help of our counselor (MFT) and her mother.

R – Reflect on what you now understand.

What new understanding does this situation leave you with?

_____

_____

_____

_____

_____

_____

Case 5: Nellie: The Case of LISTENING

Nellie is a 5-year-old girl who is described by her mother as "picky eater." Intervention started after a call from her mother in which she wanted to know if we could teach Nellie to eat. We used a protocol that helps children who have feeding and eating problems to expand their tolerance of foods by decreasing sensitivities or motor deficits, removing emotional barriers or reducing behavioral/learned habits. The first step in our intervention was to conduct a thorough sensorimotor history. This process, for Nellie and her family, revealed she had been referred to an ASD diagnostic clinic at 3 years old, and there she had received a diagnosis of receptive/expressive language disorder, not autism. Nellie's mother explained that it must have been an incorrect referral, and that Nellie couldn't be autistic because she hugged her. We continued to listen.

Nellie's mother reported that Nellie had received speech therapy to address her early language challenges and that she was happy with her progress. She had briefly received occupational therapy services to address sensory integration deficits from an experienced and respected occupational therapist. After a short period of OT, Nellie was discharged because her gross and fine motor development was basically on track. She was no longer making gains in expanding her food repertoire and the family, along with the therapist, decided to take a break from services. At the time of her discharge, her diet remained extremely limited.

In fact, it essentially consisted of nutrition drinks and one type and shape of cheesy crackers. Nellie was unable to sit at the table with others who were eating, fussing and whining when she saw or smelled other people's foods. Each week, Nellie attended two early intervention programs (comprising a schedule from 8 a.m. to 6 p.m. daily) while her parents worked. Nellie's parents reported that their primary concerns at that time were related to Nellie's increasing resistance to school attendance and that she was a picky eater. We were struck, even in the initial meeting with Nellie, by her "autistic-like" behaviors (limited eye contact, flapping, lack of joint attention, perseverative language, odd mannerisms, and repetitive play schemes). We realized we had to delve deeper and use our skills of analysis and deduction to get to the heart of the matter. Other relevant information gathered in the intake interview process included:

- Nellie's parents were recently separated.
- Nellie had several intense interests (dinosaurs, videos, trains).
- Nellie repeated phrases over and over (echolalia).
- Nellie had allergies and asthma.
- Nellie had a family history of depression and possibly undiagnosed Asperger's.
- Nellie's parents did not believe that she was on the autism spectrum.

W – What do you identify as the problem?

_____

_____

_____

_____

_____

_____

I – Isolate what you know and what you need to know.

_____

_____

_____

_____

_____

_____

What else would you want to know?

_____

_____

_____

_____

S – Strategy: Try something you think will solve the problem.

_____

_____

_____

_____

_____

_____

E – How will you Evaluate whether you successfully solved the problem you set out to solve?

_____

_____

_____

_____

_____

_____

R – Reflect on what you now understand.

_____

_____

_____

_____

_____

_____

_____

Check your thoughts against the plan we made.

W – What seems to be the problem for Nellie?

Nellie's parents perceived that her deficits had all been resolved except for remaining a "picky eater" and that she did not want to go to school. We perceived characteristics of a more complex diagnosis; namely we were highly suspicious that Nellie had autism.

I – Isolate what you know and what you need to know.

Nellie had received significant early intervention and attended a special education program for children with expressive/receptive language disorders. The information we had been given by the parents just did not match our professional observations.

S – Strategy: Try something you think will solve the problem.

We felt it was imperative that Nellie participate in a comprehensive evaluation from her insurance carrier's autism diagnostic team. In our professional opinions, this step was an essential precursor to progress. First, a formal diagnosis could give the family access to a greater variety of therapeutic interventions which, if indicated, would likely be covered by their insurance plan. More importantly, an accurate diagnosis would allow the parents to understand the needs their child had and partner with the therapeutic team to better meet developmental milestones. Once diagnosed, we would be able to effectively collaborate with Nellie's parents and provide comprehensive, yet targeted support for the members within the family system (mother, father, grandparents) in each phase of intervention.

Having the courage to take the risk of sharing our professional opinions and concerns that Nellie may have been misdiagnosed was not easy. We struggled with our own projections of how we would feel if someone said this about one of our own children. But we had to admit that, over the years, we have never heard a parent say, "I wish I had waited" or "I wish no one had ever told me." To the contrary, countless times we have been told, "I wish someone would have told me sooner." We knew Nellie's family deserved our honest recommendations. In Nellie's case, we believed that ASD may be a much more accurate diagnosis than expressive/receptive language disorder.

Although a medical diagnosis is not necessarily essential in order to begin the process of intervention, a diagnosis can remind us of the constellation of the disorder and guide the trajectory of development. A diagnosis can help us get in front of it and prevent secondary and tertiary disability.

Upon our recommendation, Nellie's parents had her reaassessed at a diagnostic clinic, and the diagnosis of Autism Spectrum Disorder (ASD) was confirmed. Once the diagnosis was given, it opened up a conversation about her readiness for kindergarten, her ability to benefit from a traditional curriculum, her need for specialized instruction, and the importance of an enriched socialization program and speech and language intervention. By empowering her parents to understand, we changed Nellie's trajectory; together we created a new plan in which challenges would be just right and she would be available for learning.

E –Evaluate whether you successfully solved the problem you set out to solve.

"Picky Eating" Nellie dramatically expanded her ability to interact with food as a result of her twice-weekly participation in food school. She will sit at the table for all meals, helping herself to a small portion of all food presented, even when she is not yet eating those foods. She does this with only minimal, intermittent fussing. She is able to touch 75 percent of all foods presented with her hands and able to touch 50 percent of food presented with her lips/mouth. She is able to "chomp" with her molars on a large variety of chewy or crunchy edible items. She chomps on veggies, fruit, cheese, beef jerky, and more.

R – Reflect on what you now understand.

Nellie is now able to lick or chomp many items, but then promptly returns them to the "spit spot," an acceptable place to deposit edible items she is not yet ready to actually swallow. She will actually eat a variety of crackers, dried fruit, and candy. She eats yogurt, applesauce, and other fruit sauces. She loves making (and drinking!) fruit smoothies. She has a much greater understanding of the "culture" of eating food. She is on her way to eating.

Although we encouraged Nellie parents to temporarily postpone her initiation into kindergarten by one year and instead pursue placement in a transitional kindergarten classroom or a year of typical preschool (not based in early intervention), her parents proceeded with placement in a general education kindergarten class. She is the youngest, smallest, and most developmentally delayed child in her classroom. However, we know that we voiced recommendations based on our clinical expertise while supporting the parents' decision to make a choice that worked within their family system.

WHY TAKE THE WISER APPROACH?

We must listen deeply, because the implications of *not* listening can be quite negative. When we don't get down to the real problem, the real heart of the matter, then children get older and the impact on them and those in their environments becomes greater, often resulting in the development of secondary and tertiary problems (bad habits).

We see older children (ages 8–18) coming in with symptoms of major anxiety, depression, and even suicidal ideation; anger; withdrawal; addiction/self-medication; poor self-image; nonadaptive, unproductive, and bad habits; unsophisticated coping strategies; and more. We understand that these symptoms often correlate with sensory integrative dysfunction.

If we don't see these older children in the latency phase, we see them as adults. They present as anxious, depressed, angry adults with poor communication, low job satisfaction, sexual dysfunction, addiction, and more.

When the older child or adult experiences a revelation about why his or her life has not "worked" (i.e., why occupational dysfunction is present), the individual often expresses relief that these difficulties may be the result of understandable and treatable roots. But they are also often discouraged because the root of the problem wasn't identified earlier, thereby potentially minimizing the secondary and tertiary symptoms that they now struggle with.

In our experience, if they had been listened to as children, and provided with more adaptive strategies earlier, then it is possible that they would be more successful at their occupation, having a better quality of a life that's meaningful and living a life in which they are more functional. They make up a story about their life, and it is not an accurate or empowering one. Denial is a powerful defense against the unknown but can become a trap if we are not careful.

It is important for parents to take the time to think about what their child struggles with, and what would help. What would create an "on-ramp" for that child look like?

We like to suggest beginning with the end in mind. What does a child need in order to be successful when he or she transitions from high school to post-secondary life (i.e, college or work)? The law requires that all children who receive special education services have a transition plan. But, in reality, all children would benefit from a transition plan. What are your child's strengths and interests? What areas are challenging to your child? Make a plan to support the interests and resolve the weaknesses. Although it sounds simple, it is surprising how many parents wait or overlook this strategy. Consider the case of Mary Jo.

Mary Jo's older brother loves sports, but Mary Jo loves to read and the only sport she's willing to participate in is hiking. She's a bit clumsy and struggles to make friends at school, mostly because she doesn't share the same interests as her school peers. She likes science fiction/fantasy books, movies, and likes to write her own stories. She enjoys cooking and is interested in being "green" (she can be militant about recycling and water usage). She says, "No one likes the books I like—they're morons." Mary Jo has complained of this since elementary school, and the refrain continues now that she has entered seventh grade. She is quite isolated and increasingly doesn't want to leave the house. Mary Jo's parents are concerned she is becoming depressed.

What does this child need? It is likely that Mary Jo needs to find peers. How? Parents need to help her identify what she finds interesting (ecology, environmental science, science fiction/fantasy genre, writing) and engage in the social opportunities where she can meet like-minded individuals (intellectual peers). What ideas come to mind? Consider ComicCon events in the area, a writing class at a local bookstore, events posted at the local comic book stores, finding a local author for Mary Jo to interview/be mentored by, participate in events sponsored by Green Peace or REI or the Appalachian Mountain Club. Can she volunteer at the local library? Finding the opportunities for Mary Jo to be engaged in her areas of interests will help her meet others who share her interests and, by doing so, help her develop social skills as well as the habits needed for post-secondary employment.

Children provide us with wisdom. If we can develop the skills of an architect, we can decipher their message and help to create strong foundations to optimal health, well-being, and social participation. Being an observer of oneself, one's child, and the world in which we live can give us a blueprint for building a better life. It's time: Open the door to a sensational life for yourself and your family.

Bibliography

Ahn, R. R., Miller, L. J., Milberger, S., & McIntosh, D. N. (2004). Prevalence of parents' perceptions of sensory processing disorders among kindergarten children. *American Journal of Occupational Therapy, 58,* 287–293.

Antonovsky A. Unraveling the mystery of health. How people manage stress and stay well. San Francisco: Jossey-Bass, 1987.

Antonovsky, A. (1987). Sense of coherence scale in unraveling the mystery of health. In *How People Manage Stress and Stay Well.* San Francisco: Jossey-Bass.

Antonovsky, A. (1996). The salutogenic model as a theory to guide health promotion. *Health Promotion International, 11*(1), 11–18.

Ayres, A. J. (2005). *Sensory Integration and the Child.* Los Angeles: Western Psychological Services.

Baker, A. E. Z., Lane, A., Angley, M. T., & Young, R. L. (2008). The relationship between sensory processing patterns and behavioral responsiveness in autistic disorder: A pilot study. *Journal of Autism and Related Disorders, 38,* 867–875.

Baranek, G. T. (2002). Efficacy of sensory and motor interventions for children with autism. *Journal of Autism and Related Disorders, 32*(5), 397–422.

Boyd, B. A. (2002). Examining the relationship between stress and lack of social support in mothers of children with autism. *Focus on Autism and Other Developmental Disabilities, 17,* 208–215.

Boyle, C. A., Boulet, S., et al. (2011). Trends in the prevalence of developmental disabilities in U.S. children, 1997–2008. *Pediatrics, 127,* 1034–1042. *http://dx.doi.org/10.1542/peds.2010-2989.*

Brown, C. E., & Dunn, W. (2002). *Adolescent/Adult Sensory Profile User's Manual.* : Psychological Corporation, A Harcourt Assessment Company.

Bronfenbrenner, U. (1986). Ecology of the family as a context for human development: Research perspectives. *Developmental Psychology,* 22, 723–742

Cacioppo, J. T., Hughes, M. E., Waite, L. J., Hawkley, L. C., & Thisted, R. A. (2006). Loneliness as a specific risk factor for depressive symptoms: Cross-sectional and longitudinal analyses. *Psychology and Aging, 21*(1), 140–151. *http://dx.doi.org/10.1037/0882-7974.21.1.140.*

Cacioppo, J., & Patrick, W. (2009). *Loneliness: Human Nature and the Need for Social Connection.* New York: W. W. Norton.

Centers for Disease Control and Prevention. (n.d.). *Key findings: Trends in the prevalence of developmental disabilities in U. S. children, 1997–2008.* Retrieved from *http://www.cdc. gov/ncbddd/features/birthdefects-dd-keyfindings.html.*

Cohn, E., Miller, L. J, & Tickle-Degnen, L. (2000). Parental hopes for therapy outcomes: Children with sensory modulation disorders. *American Journal of Occupational Therapy 54*(1), 36–43.

Freedman, B., & Whitney, R. (2011). Family quality of life. *Sensory Focus, 8,* 8–13.

Gibbs, V. (2013). *Self-Regulation in Children: Keeping the Body, Mind & Emotions on Task in Children with Autism, ADHD or Sensory Disorders.* PESI Video Webcast.

Green, S. A. & Ben-Sasson, A. (2010). Anxiety disorders and sensory overresponsivity in children with autism spectrum disorders: Is there a causal relationship? *Journal of Autism and Developmental Disorders.* doi: 201010.1007/s10803-010-1007-x.

Heiman, T., & Berger, O. (2008). Parents of children with Asperger syndrome or learning disabilities: Family environment and social support. *Research in Developmental Disabilities, 29,* 289–300.

Hoffman, L., Marquis, J., Poston, D., Summers, J. A., & Turnbull, A. (2006). Assessing family outcomes: Psychometric evaluation of the Beach Center Family Quality of Life Scale. *Journal of Marriage and Family, 68,* 1069–1083.

Kinnealey, M., Koenig, K., & Smith, S. (2011). Relationships between sensory modulation and social supports and health-related quality of life. *American Journal of Occupational Therapy,* 65, 320–327. doi:10.5014/ ajot.2011.001370

Knox, S. (1974). A play scale. In M. Reilly (Ed.), *Play as Exploratory Learning.* Beverly Hills, CA: Sage.

Kramer, P. & Hinojosa, J. (2009). *Frames of Reference for Pediatric Occupational Therapy,* 3rd ed. Philadelphia: Lippincott, Williams & Wilkins.

Lane, A., Young, R. L, Baker, A. E., & Angley, M. (2010). Sensory processing subtypes in autism: Association with adaptive behavior. *Journal of Autism and Developmental Disorders, 40,* 112–122.

Larson, E. (2000) Mothering: Letting go of the past ideal and valuing the real. *American Journal of Occupational Therapy, 54*(3), 249–251.

Law, M., Cooper, B., Strong, S., Stewart, D., Rigby, P., & Letts, L. (1996). The Person-Environment-Occupation Model: A transactive approach to occupational performance. *Canadian Journal of Occupational Therapy, 63,* 9–23.

Lee, L., Harrington, R., Louie, B., & Newschaffer, C. (2008). Children with autism: Quality of life and parental concerns. *Journal of Autism and Developmental Disorders, 38,* 1147–1160.

May-Benson, T. A., & Koomar, J. A., (2010). Systematic review of the research evidence examining the effectiveness of interventions using a sensory integrative approach for children. *American Journal of Occupational Therapy, 3,* 403–414.

McLaughlin, D. P., & Harrison, C. A. (2006). Parenting practices of mothers of children with ADHD: The role of maternal and child factors. *Child and Adolescent Mental Health, 11,* 82–88.

Mee, J., Sumsion, T., & Craik, C. (2004). Mental health clients confirm the value of occupation in building competence and self-identify. *British Journal of Occupational Therapy, 31,* 225–233.

Miller, L. J., & Lane, S. J. (2000). Toward a consensus in terminology in sensory integration theory and practice: Part 1: Taxonomy of neurophysiological process. *Sensory Integration Special Interest Section, 23*(1), 1–4.

Miller, L. J., Schoen, S. A., James, K., & Schaaf, R. C. (2007). Lessons learned: A pilot study on occupational therapy effectiveness for children with sensory processing disorders. *American Journal of Occupational Therapy, 61,* 161–169.

Nakamura, W., Stewart, K., & Tatarka, M. E. (1993). Assessing father-infant interactions using the NCAST Teaching Scale: A pilot study. *American Journal of Occupational Therapy, 54*(1), 44–51.

Nettles, S. M., Mucherah, W., & Jones, D. S. (2000). Understanding resilience: The role of social resources. *Journal of Education for Students Placed at Risk, 5*(1–2), 47–60.

Olson, J., & Esdaile, S. (2000). Mothering young children with disabilities in a challenging urban environment. *American Journal of Occupational Therapy, 54*(3), 307–314.

Pfeiffer, B. Kinnealey, M., Reed, D., & Herzbert, G. (2005). Sensory modulation and affective disorders in children and adolescents with Asperger's disorder. *American Journal of Occupational Therapy, 59*(3), 335–345.

Primeau, L. (1998). A orchestration of work and play within families. *American Journal of Occupational Therapy, 52*(3), 188–195.

Lane, S.J, Reynolds, S., & Thacker, L. (2010). Sensory Overresponsivity and ADHD: Differentiating Using Electrodermal Responses, Cortisol, and Anxiety. *Frontiers in Integrative Neuroscience. 4*(8). doi: 10.3389/fnint.2010.00008

Rogers, S. J. & Ozonoff, S. (2005). Annotation: What do we know about sensory dysfunction in autism? A critical review of the empirical evidence. *Journal of Child Psychology and Psychiatry, and Allied Disciplines, 46,* 1255–1268.

Schaaf, R., Schoen, S. A., Smith Roley, S., Lane, S., Koomar, J., & May-Benson, T. A. (2009). A frame of reference for sensory integration. In Kramer, P. & Hinojosa, J. *Frames of Reference for Pediatric Occupational Therapy,* 3rd ed. Philadelphia: Lippincott, Williams & Wilkins.

Schaaf, R., & Burke, J. (1997). *What Happens When We Play? A Neurodevelopmental Explanation in the Essence of Play.* Bethesda, MD: AOTA.

Schaaf, R., Toth-Cohen, S., Johnson, S., Outten, G., & Benevides, T. (2011). The everyday routines of families of children with autism: Examining the impact of sensory processing difficulties on the family. *Autism, 15*(3), 373–389.

Schaaf, R. C. (2011). Interventions that address sensory dysfunction for individuals with autism spectrum disorders: Preliminary evidence for the superiority of sensory integration compared to other sensory approaches. In Volkmar, F., Cicchetti, D., Reichow, B., & Doehring, P. (Eds). *Evidence-Based Practices in Autism Spectrum Disorders*. New York: Springer.

Strong, S., Rigby, P., Stewart, D., Law, M., Letts, L., & Cooper, B. (1999). Application of the Person-Environment-Occupation Model: A practical tool. *Canadian Journal of Occupational Therapy, 66*, 122–133.

Tomchek, S. D., & Dunn, W. (2007). Sensory processing in children with and without autism: A comparative study using the Short Sensory Profile. *American Journal of Occupational Therapy, 61*, 190–200.

Toomey, K. (n.d). *Picky Eaters v. Problem Eaters: The S.O.S. Approach to Feeding*, retrieved March 24, 2014 from http://www.sosapproach-conferences.com.

Whitney, R. (2008). *Nonverbal Learning Disorder*. New York: Perigee Books.

Whitney, R. (2010). S.N.O.T. Protocol. In Morris, K. (Ed). *Insights into Sensory Issues for Professionals*. Arlington, TX: Sensory World.

Whitney, R., & Gibbs, V. (2013). *Raising Kids with Sensory Processing Disorders: A Week-by-Week Guide to Solving Everyday Sensory Issues*. Waco, TX: Prufrock Press.

Whitney, R. & Miller Kuhaneck, H. (In press). Diagnostic Statistical Manual V changes to the autism diagnostic criteria: A critical moment for occupational therapists. *Online Journal of Occupational Therapy*.

Recommended Readings and Resources

Bartl, A. (2008). *101 Relaxation Games for Children: Finding a Little Peace and Quiet in Between.* Alameda, CA: Hunter House, Inc.

Biel, L., & Peske, N. (2009). *Raising a Sensory Smart Child: The Definitive Handbook for Helping your Child with Sensory Integration Issues.* New York: Penguin.

Branzei, S., & Keely, J. (1995). *Grossology: The Science of Really Gross Things.* New York: Penguin Putnam. *http://www.grossology.org/.*

Brooks, R. Resilience, Motivation and Family Relationships. *http://www.drrobertbrooks.com/.*

Curtis, S. E. (2008). *Understanding your Child's Puzzling Behavior: A Guide for Parents of Children with Behavioral, Social and Learning Challenges.* Bainbridge Island, WA: Lifespan Press.

de Saint Exupery, A. (1968). *The Little Prince.* New York: Harcourt Childrens Books.

Dunn, W. (2007). *Living Sensationally.* London: Jessica Kingsley Publishers.

Family Fun magazine. http://www.parents.com/familyfun-magazine/.

Henry Occupational Therapy Services (wonderful guides for home and classroom). http://www.ateachabout.com/.

How Does Your Engine Run? Therapyworks program. *www.alertprogram.com.*

Kaye, P. (1991). *Games for Learning.* New York: Farrar, Straus, and Giroux.

Kaye, Peggy. (1991). *Games for Learning.* New York: HarperCollins.

Kranowitz, C. (2001). *Answers to Questions Teachers Ask about Sensory Integration.* Arlington, TX: Future Horizons.

Milne, A. A. (2001). *Winnie-the-Pooh.* New York: Penguin Group.

Notbohm, E., & Zysk, V. (2010). *1001 Great Ideas for Teaching and Raising Children with Autism or Asperger's.* Arlington, TX: Future Horizons.

Seligman, M. E. (2007). *The Optimistic Child.* New York: Houghton Mifflin Harcourt.

Sensational Processing Disorder Foundation. www.sinetwork.org.

Sensory World magazines. www.sifocus.org.

Shure, M., & Foy DiGeronimo, T. (1996). *How to Raise a Thinking Child.* New York: Gallery Books.

Toomey, K. (n.d). *Picky Eaters v. Problem Eaters: The S.O.S. Approach to Feeding,* retrieved March 24, 2014 from http://www.sosapproach-conferences.com.

Trott, Colby. (2002). *Oh Behave!* Alexandria, VA: Psychological Corporation.

Follow and share your experiences with the WISER approach

---

www.ittakesthevillage.net

APPENDIX

Worksheets * Activities * Journals * Guides

- Examples of Questions for the Transactional Influences Within The Families
- Coping Strategies Journals
- All I Need To Know I Learned When I Was On The Playground
- Seven Guiding Principles for Success
- Gotta Get A Dose of Sensation
- Are You A Tigger? Pooh? Eeyore? Owl or Rabbit?
- Activities for Vestibular and Proprioceptive Learning
- Activities for Visual System
- Activities for Tactile
- Activities for Olfactory/Gustatory
- Activities for Auditory
- If it Takes a Village, Who Does What?
- Sensational Tool Kit
- Treatment Planning
- The WISER Approach Worksheet
- The SNOT Protocol

Examples of Questions for the Transactional Influences Within the Family

Family Interaction

1. How often do you have meals together as a family?

_____

_____

_____

2. Can you and your child share ideas or talk about things that really matter? Do your children share time and ideas together?

_____

_____

_____

3. Do you have a regular family game night, go for walks, or have other social activities you enjoy doing together?

_____

_____

_____

Quality of Parents' Relationship

4. Do you and your partner share enough alone time together? How would you rate the quality of that time together (1 = not satisfied at all, 5 = extremely satisfied)?

_____

_____

_____

5. Do you feel satisfied with your relationship with your partner?

_____

_____

_____

6. Can you name three things your partner did yesterday to care for you or your family?

_____

_____

_____

Support for Person with Disability

7. Can you name three people you can ask to help you even if they would have to go out of their way to do so?

_____

_____

_____

8. Would you say each member of your family participates in at least one club or enjoyable activity (i.e., plays tennis, member of a Boy Scout troop, plays soccer, mom has a girls night out)?

_____

_____

_____

9. Are you able to manage arranging the family's medical services or other social events without getting overly stressed?

_____

_____

_____

Material Well-Being

10. During past six months, has anyone in the family changed a job because of problems related to child care?

_____

_____

_____

11. During the past month, have you had to leave work because the school was unable to manage your child's behavior?

_____

_____

_____

12. Are you employed at the level you would like to be?

_____

_____

_____

Physical and Emotional Well-Being

Physical

13. Would you say you and your partner get at least 20 minutes of exercise two times a week?

_____

_____

_____

14. Does anyone inside or outside the home smoke?

_____

_____

_____

15. In general, would you say you get enough sleep?

_____

_____

_____

Emotional

16. In general, do you feel the school does not have to contact you about your child's problems?

_____

_____

_____

17. Can you name three people with whom you can talk about matters that are important to you?

_____

_____

_____

18. Do you feel loved by you family, immediate or extended?

_____

_____

_____

Parenting

19. Can you read, tell stories, sing songs or otherwise interact with your child daily in satisfying ways?

_____

_____

_____

20. All things considered, would you say you can cope pretty well with the demands of parenthood?

_____

_____

_____

21. Does your child spend just as much time alone without supervision as other children his/her age?

_____

_____

_____

Questionnaire created and copyrighted by Rondalyn V. Whitney, PhD, OTR/L

What Coping Strategies Would You Use?

Response	Primary Sensory Strategy
	• Olfactory • Tactile • Auditory • Proprioception/Deep pressure • Visual • Movement • Oral/Gustatory
	• Olfactory • Tactile • Auditory • Proprioception/Deep pressure • Visual • Movement • Oral/Gustatory
	• Olfactory • Tactile • Auditory • Proprioception/Deep pressure • Visual • Movement • Oral/Gustatory
	• Olfactory • Tactile • Auditory • Proprioception/Deep pressure • Visual • Movement • Oral/Gustatory

All I Need to Know I Learned When I Was on the Playground . . .

When you're on the merry-go-round and Pat makes it too fast, hang on before trying to tell him to slow down.

> Translated: Sometimes life moves faster than you'd like, but you can't exit when you're in the fast lane.

The most fun in life I've ever had was in the back of a line where the folks were "all in the same boat" rather than having to look over their shoulders for "encroachers."

> Translated: You don't always have to be first in line to have the best time.

When you bail out of a swing, you can break your arm like Yogi did.

> Translated: Think before you leap and learn from the mistakes of others.

When you are on the monkey bars as a first grader, you can get better (like the third graders) if you persist.

> Translated: Someone else is always older and wiser, but if you keep at it, you'll get better too.

If you need help, find a grown-up like in the *Sally, Dick and Jane* stories.

> Translated: You don't have to know it all (Whew!).

No one wants to play with a bad sport, even when you're the one who was right.

> Translated: Be a bad sport and be lonely.

When someone takes their marbles and goes home, no one gets to play.

Translated: Sharing makes life more fun for everyone.

The kid who helps you when the ball goes in the bushes makes the best partner in the math project.

Translated: Real friends are friends in each area, not just when it's convenient.

It's not always your turn unless you play by yourself.

Translated: Patience.

Modulation Ideas

Profile	Observed Behavior	Program
Sensory overresponsive (SOR)	Uncooperative Tantrum Fight/Fight/Fright/Freeze	Deep pressure Slow rocking Low-tone sound (like bass drums, flute, piano)
Sensory underresponsive (SUR)	Sluggish Slow to transition Low attention	Interactive metronome Exercise Fast music, high tone (violins, *Star Wars* soundtrack)
Sensory seeking/Craving (SS/C)	Touching excessively Making noise for the sake of noise Bumping objects Crashing	Combine intense input with organizing input Run in fast circles, then do five push ups Jump up and down then freeze like a statute
Overload! (Avoidant, seeker, or underresponder experiences too much input)	Uncooperative Tantrum Fight/Fight/Fright/Freeze	Use calming and organizing strategies Remove input (low lights, quite calming music) Think about each of the senses!

Seven Guiding Principles for Success

Context Influencing Behavioral Responses				
Parenting skill	Teacher expectations	Peer interactions	Sensation in the environment	Internal state (fatigue, hunger, etc.)

1. **Mind the gap: Developmental vs. chronological ages.** Even though a child is, say, 7 years old, it is common for him or her to have (for example) fine motor skills consistent with a 9-year-old and gross motor skills of a 6-year-old! Our family both bequeaths and incubates various talents for our children. Think about the developmental ability of the child. No child develops each skill simultaneously; some gain cognitive skills before motor, and others vice versa. Girls tend to develop fine motor and language skills 1–2 years ahead of their male peers, while boys tend to gain gross motor and visual motor skills 1–2 years ahead of their female peers. Socially, children develop skills of collaboration, then cooperation; by end of the 4th grade, most are developmentally ready for the challenge of competition.

2. **Behavior happens for a reason.** We have to become detectives to see why a child is behaving in a certain way. Cling to the belief that children WANT to be good and set out to find what barriers are present that are causing the them to be unable to meet their innate goal.

3. **Check the triangle.** Looking at the environment: the sensory processing skills, the developmental skill level and expectations of the task can help you detect what is "hiding in

the background" of both desirable and undesirable behavior. The environment (and you are part of the equation), the occupation, and the child interact in a dynamic way with each leg of the triangle available for adjustment. 1) environment, 2) occupation, and 3) the child = 3

4. **Whose problem is it?** When problem solving, ask yourself this question. For example, a messy house is often the parent's problem, right? How can you partner with the parents to create motivation for the child, while helping the parents solve the problem? A mess becomes a problem for a child if the items disappear for a week when Mom cleans it up!

5. **Think about the anatomy of an upset.** Why do you (the adult) get upset? We all get upset for one of these reasons (a) we have an unfilled expectation; (b) we have a thwarted intention; or (c) we have an undelivered communication. Think about it: (a) you expected a bracelet for your birthday but got packing tape and batteries from your husband; (b) you want to drive to the store but you encounter a traffic jam; and (c) you are frustrated that your mom is in your kitchen making a pie when you want to remove sugar from your diet, but you can't tell her because it would hurt her feelings. Take on the challenge of exploring why you are upset and see whether you can resolve one of the three barriers: (a) reassess your expectations, (b) reexamine your intentions, or (c) communicate in a satisfying way.

6. **Develop a feelings vocabulary.** We all need to express ourselves and understand how we feel. If we are always only "fine," we fail to convey the truth of feeling angry, peeved, irritated, furious, or explosive! We lose the opportunity to express that we feel good, happy, or excited. We are unable to use language that explains apprehension, fear, or terror. Work as a family to develop a way to express a range of emotions. Perhaps make lists of words that relate to a feeling, post them, and have your child work with you to put them in order of least to most emotive. You can use a thermometer (with cool temperature words and fevered emotions). Expressing emotions has been shown in the research to reduce stress, promote health and well-being, and improve function across many settings (both negative and positive emotions). So, get those out emotions OUT!

7. **Practice authentic apologies.** Dr. Randy Pausch left us with many important messages in his *Last Lecture*, but the one that brings magic into the daily lives of families is the steps of an apology. To be a TRUE apology one should say, "I'm sorry. It was all my fault. What can I do to make it up to you?" Teach children to apologize. Practice apologizing yourself—you set an important example.

Gotta Get a Dose of Sensation!

Area in Need of Development	Games to Support Development of Abilities
Flexible thinking	• The Set • Ghosts Blitz • Iota (the big game in a teeny tin and the teeniest person goes first) • Caves and Claws • Quarto
Fine motor	• Zoo Sticks • Kerplunk • Pick up sticks • Bathtub finger paint • Stringing beads, knitting, Rainbow Looms
Gross motor	• Sit and spin • Jump rope • Balloon games • Musical dusting (Put on some music and socks, hand out dust cloths and dust while doing the twist!)
Regulation	• Heavy work (exercise, carry in groceries, stomp and flatten empty boxes) • Start and Stop (run around, wiggle, be silly while 20 seconds of music plays, then stop the music, freeze, and begin again) • One minute of mindfulness • Make a list of what you are grateful for
Handwriting	• Write three treats on the grocery list • Write a thank you note each week for something you're grateful for • Make breadsticks or cookies in the shape of letters • Knit or use a Rainbow Loom
Develop helpful habits	• Balloon chores (write a chore on the balloon with a marker and the child selects the balloon. Once the chore is done, they get to pop the balloon!) • One-minute chores • Peel vegetables with a vegetable peeler • Help with dishes each night
Practice persistence	• Make a plan for sticking to something hard each month and celebrate when you do!

Are You a Tigger?

Tigger types are the Seekers and Speakers. They need us to provide them with some room to bounce, kick, wiggle, squirm, talk it out, and run it out. We need to feed their need for sensation!

To balance the scales, you can try to. . .

- Take frequent wiggle breaks.
- Intensify foods with spices and texture; drink fizzy things through a straw.
- Shake it up! Try new routes! Move the furniture!
- Listen to music, chew gum, and have fidgets on your desk.
- Add bubbles to your bath.
- Blow on whistles.

_____

_____

_____

_____

Reflections for Tiggers

I tried _____   I felt _____.
I tried _____   I felt _____.
I tried _____   I felt _____.
I tried _____   I felt _____.
I tried _____   I felt _____.
I tried _____   I felt _____.

Notes to myself:

_____

_____

_____

_____

Your Assignment: Make Up a Game

What sensory system will you use?

_____
_____
_____
_____

What materials will you select?

_____
_____
_____
_____

When will you use it?

_____
_____
_____
_____

What part of the academic curriculum does this game connect to?

_____
_____
_____
_____

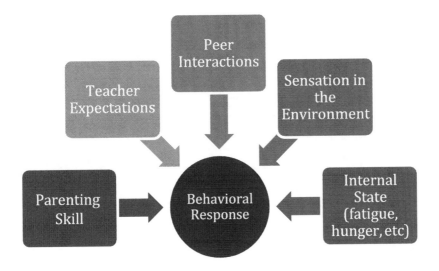

Behavior:

Other factors that may be contributing:

My plan for detective work:

What I learned I can use for future behavioral responses:

Are You a Pooh?

Pooh types are easily bothered. To balance the scales, we need to help eliminate the extraneous and make their life predictable. They tend to like deep pressure and not tickly touches.

To balance the scales, you can try to...

- Shop at boutiques and online, not in the malls.
- Select foods by texture and color.
- Know your limits, and use routines to feel organized.
- Only change one thing at a time, and give yourself time to adapt or see if you like it.
- Buy more than one item of your favorite article of clothing; buy in multiple colors.

_____

_____

_____

_____

_____

Reflections for Poohs

I tried _____   I felt _____.
I tried _____   I felt _____.
I tried _____   I felt _____.
I tried _____   I felt _____.
I tried _____   I felt _____.
I tried _____   I felt _____.

Notes to myself:

_____

_____

_____

_____

_____

Your Assignment: Make Up a Game

What sensory system will you use?

_____

_____

_____

_____

_____

What materials will you select?

_____

_____

_____

_____

_____

When will you use it?

_____

_____

_____

_____

What part of the academic curriculum does this game connect to?

_____

_____

_____

_____

_____

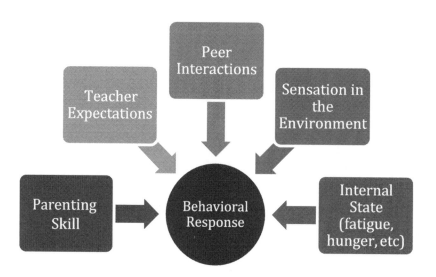

Behavior:

Other factors that may be contributing:

My plan for detective work:

What I learned I can use for future behavioral responses:

Are You an Eeyore?

Eeyores were glad when McDonalds *finally* added "Warning: Contents of this cup may be extremely hot" to their cups. They need you to turn things up a bit, but slowly.

To balance the scales, you can try to. . .

- Find ways to alert yourself to the environment.
  (You may need more than you think; you may feel overwhelmed by the time you get enough.)
- Eliminate scatter rugs; install guard rails.
- Take little sips of hot drinks/food to test the temperature.
- Strengthen your resilience (but get our attention first).
- Add one challenge at a time, and make sure you understand the expectations.
- Build your muscles.
- Remind people to be kind to you and that you're doing your best.

_____

_____

_____

_____

Reflections for Eeyores

I tried _____   I felt _____.
I tried _____   I felt _____.
I tried _____   I felt _____.
I tried _____   I felt _____.
I tried _____   I felt _____.
I tried _____   I felt _____.

Notes to myself:

_____

_____

_____

Your Assignment: Make Up a Game

What sensory system will you use?

_____

_____

_____

_____

_____

What materials will you select?

_____

_____

_____

_____

_____

When will you use it?

_____

_____

_____

_____

_____

What part of the academic curriculum does this game connect to?

_____

_____

_____

_____

_____

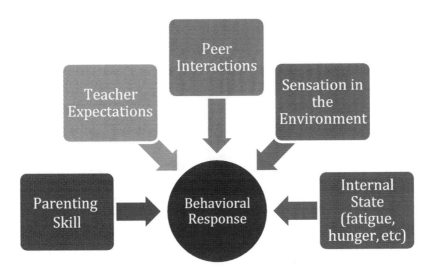

Behavior:

_____

Other factors that may be contributing:

_____

My plan for detective work:

_____

What I learned I can use for future behavioral responses:

_____

Are You an Owl & Rabbit?

You need to know people will honor your *need* for self-protection! You can feel really scared if too much sensation comes your way.

To balance the scales, you can try to...

- Use checklists, and stick to routines and schedules.
- Tell others to prep you well ahead of time for any changes and that surprises are upsetting to you!
- Learn what sensory input feels safe. Find a brand, scent, or strategy and stick to it (and advocate for yourself).
- Set up your space to reduce sensory input (simplicity and order are your friends).
- Let people in on the secret that you feel scared when you look uncooperative. Practice saying, "That would make me feel uncomfortable" rather than "No."

_____

_____

_____

_____

Reflections for Owls & Rabbits

I tried _____ I felt _____.

I tried _____ I felt _____.

I tried _____ I felt _____.

I tried _____ I felt _____.

I tried _____ I felt _____.

I tried _____ I felt _____.

Notes to myself:

_____

_____

Your Assignment: Make Up a Game

What sensory system will you use?

_____

_____

_____

_____

_____

What materials will you select?

_____

_____

_____

_____

_____

When will you use it?

_____

_____

_____

_____

_____

What part of the academic curriculum does this game connect to?

_____

_____

_____

_____

_____

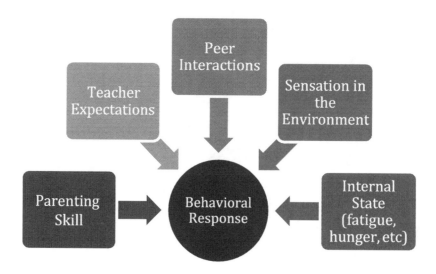

Behavior:

Other factors that may be contributing:

My plan for detective work:

What I learned I can use for future behavioral responses:

On the following pages, you will find activities for each sensory system, a journal page with prompts to help you reflect on a child's behavior and a scientific approach to understanding that behavior. In additional you will find page which you can record various activities/ interventions you discover are helping in promoting optimal engagement in family and social life. We have also included a page to encourage you to consider creating a game that will help your child develop skills or enjoy the sensation of each sensory system, tactile, olfactory, etc.

Activities for Vestibular and Proprioceptive Learning

1. Sit on a therapy ball when doing homework.

2. Lay over a therapy ball when watching TV.

3. Swing and play on playground equipment.

4. Run, kick a ball, hit a ball, do cartwheels.

5. Bend over and pick up clothes off the floor.

6. Help with yard work.

7. Water the flowers.

8. Bring in the groceries.

9. Carry or push the laundry basket.

Journal Use the scientific method and become an aggressive researcher for your child.	
What I observe . . . (no judgments here; must pass the stranger test)	
My hypothesis (hunger, fear/ anxiety, sensory, cognitive, other)	
Method to test out your hypothesis	
Data:	
My working theory and future directions	

My activities for Vestibular and Proprioceptive Learning:

_____

_____

_____

_____

_____

_____

_____

_____

_____

_____

_____

_____

_____

_____

_____

_____

_____

_____

_____

_____

_____

_____

_____

Activities for Visual System

1. Find the hidden puzzle pieces under the couch cushions.

2. Make letters out of cereal or popcorn pieces.

3. Instead of telephone tag, play texting tag and send a message on your friend' phone back to the next friend. Ex: C+A+T or YR A BFF.

4. Play I-Spy with a homemade telescope, periscope, or binoculars.

5. Use a coupon at the grocery store, match it to the item on a shelf.

6. Set the table.

7. Estimate! Think about how many socks will fit into the drawer, how many grapes in the Ziploc bag, etc.

8. Treasure hunt: Plan a party or family game night and hide the bag of chips, cookies, juice all over the house or the yard! Use small clues or hints for the children. Whoever finds the flyer for the pizza delivery company gets to pick out the first topping

Journal Use the scientific method and become an aggressive researcher for your child.	
What I observe . . . (no judgments here; must pass the stranger test)	
My hypothesis (hunger, fear/ anxiety, sensory, cognitive, other)	
Method to test out your hypothesis	
Data:	
My working theory and future directions	

My activities for Vestibular and Proprioceptive Learning:

Activities for Tactile

1. Get messy with art!
2. Mix some food for dinner.
3. Name hidden objects in a box of rice (no peeking).
4. Play dress up.
5. Play with bubbles in the bath.
6. Wear a boa or a scarf when doing your homework (or working on your taxes—really, try it).
7. Have a finger food dinner party.
8. Drink through straws (even pudding and applesauce).

Journal
Use the scientific method and become an aggressive researcher for your child.

What I observe . . . (no judgments here; must pass the stranger test)	
My hypothesis (hunger, fear/ anxiety, sensory, cognitive, other)	
Method to test out your hypothesis	
Data:	
My working theory and future directions	

My activities for Vestibular and Proprioceptive Learning:

_____

_____

_____

_____

_____

_____

_____

_____

_____

_____

_____

_____

_____

_____

_____

_____

_____

_____

_____

_____

_____

_____

_____

_____

_____

Activities For Olfactory/Gustatory

1. Get messy with food! (also tactile)
2. Go for a walk and smell the roses!
3. Close your eyes and play I-Spy with your nose (you can tuck scented cotton balls into cleaned out ketchup bottles and "squeeze" the scents out).
4. Have a tasting party: Organize the tastes by your taste buds (salty, sweet, etc.) or texture (crunch, smooth, grainy, etc.).
5. Hide-and-seek smells; Hide a smell—who can find the stinky sock?

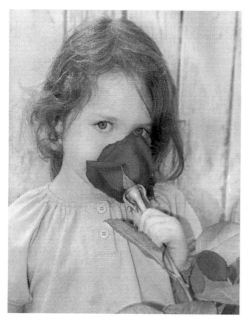

| **Journal** |
| **Use the scientific method and become an aggressive researcher for your child.** |

What I observe . . . (no judgments here; must pass the stranger test)	
My hypothesis (hunger, fear/ anxiety, sensory, cognitive, other)	
Method to test out your hypothesis	
Data:	
My working theory and future directions	

My activities for Visual System:

_____

_____

_____

_____

_____

_____

_____

_____

_____

_____

_____

_____

_____

_____

_____

_____

_____

_____

_____

_____

_____

_____

_____

_____

Activities For Auditory

1. Play "I Spy" with your ears. Instead of I Spy something red you might say "I hear something banging." Tune in to sounds in nature or around the house.

2. Mix a play list for different tasks (music for homework, music for bedtime, etc.)

3. Play guessing games with sounds; make a sound and see if you can guess it. For example, if I made the sound of a wolf, could you guess it?

4. Play with whistles and kazoos, or blow into water to make sounds like when in the bath.

5. Have a jam night. Drag out spoons and pans and play a song (like they do in the movie *Tarzan*).

6. Talk in accents.

7. Play music during dinner or have a quiet dinner.

8. Play a listening game. Listen for mistakes (I went to the store and bought a horse; I'm going up the steps [when you are walking down]).

Journal **Use the scientific method and become an aggressive researcher for your child.**	
What I observe . . . (no judgments here; must pass the stranger test)	
My hypothesis (hunger, fear/ anxiety, sensory, cognitive, other)	
Method to test out your hypothesis	
Data:	
My working theory and future directions	

My activities for Tactile:

_____

_____

_____

_____

_____

_____

_____

_____

_____

_____

_____

_____

_____

_____

_____

_____

_____

_____

_____

_____

_____

_____

_____

_____

If it takes a village, who does what?	
Medical team (physician assistant, pediatrician, nurse practitioner, psychiatrist)	
Psychologist	
Marriage and family therapist	
Occupational therapists	
Audiologist	
Optometrist	
Physical therapist	
Educational therapists	
Tutor	
General education teacher	
Special education teacher	
Behaviorists	
Family navigator/Parent coach	
Educational consultant	
Other	

Your Ideas Here . . . for Treatment Planning:	
Make dinner a sensory sensitive act	
Make cleaning up a spill a sensory sensitive act	
Make bedtime routine a sensory sensitive act	
Make laundry a sensory sensitive act	
Make morning routine a sensory sensitive act	
Make school work a sensory sensitive act	
Make bed time a sensory sensitive act	

*See Winnie Dunn's book Living Sensationally for more sensational ideas.

Sensational Tool Kit	
Olfactory	
Visual	
Proprioceptive	
Gustatory	
Tactile	
Deep pressure	
Auditory	
Movement	

The WISER Approach

<u>W</u>hat is the problem we need to solve?

<u>I</u>solate what you know and what you need to know

<u>S</u>trategy: Give one a try

<u>E</u>valuate whether your strategy solved the right problem

<u>R</u>eflect on what you now understand

The WISER Approach

<u>W</u>hat is the problem we need to solve?

<u>I</u>solate what you know and what you need to know

<u>S</u>trategy: Give one a try

<u>E</u>valuate whether your strategy solved the right problem

<u>R</u>eflect on what you now understand

The WISER Approach

<u>W</u>hat is the problem we need to solve?

<u>I</u>solate what you know and what you need to know

<u>S</u>trategy: Give one a try

<u>E</u>valuate whether your strategy solved the right problem

<u>R</u>eflect on what you now understand

The WISER Approach

<u>W</u>hat is the problem we need to solve?

<u>I</u>solate what you know and what you need to know

<u>S</u>trategy: Give one a try

<u>E</u>valuate whether your strategy solved the right problem

<u>R</u>eflect on what you now understand

The WISER Approach

__W__hat is the problem we need to solve?

__I__solate what you know and what you need to know

__S__trategy: Give one a try

__E__valuate whether your strategy solved the right problem

__R__eflect on what you now understand

The WISER Approach

<u>W</u>hat is the problem we need to solve?

<u>I</u>solate what you know and what you need to know

<u>S</u>trategy: Give one a try

<u>E</u>valuate whether your strategy solved the right problem

<u>R</u>eflect on what you now understand

The WISER Approach

_____

<u>W</u>hat is the problem we need to solve?

_____

<u>I</u>solate what you know and what you need to know

_____

<u>S</u>trategy: Give one a try

_____

<u>E</u>valuate whether your strategy solved the right problem

_____

<u>R</u>eflect on what you now understand

_____

The WISER Approach

<u>W</u>hat is the problem we need to solve?

<u>I</u>solate what you know and what you need to know

<u>S</u>trategy: Give one a try

<u>E</u>valuate whether your strategy solved the right problem

<u>R</u>eflect on what you now understand

The WISER Approach

<u>W</u>hat is the problem we need to solve?

<u>I</u>solate what you know and what you need to know

<u>S</u>trategy: Give one a try

<u>E</u>valuate whether your strategy solved the right problem

<u>R</u>eflect on what you now understand

The WISER Approach

<u>W</u>hat is the problem we need to solve?

<u>I</u>solate what you know and what you need to know

<u>S</u>trategy: Give one a try

<u>E</u>valuate whether your strategy solved the right problem

<u>R</u>eflect on what you now understand

The SNOT Protocol

Occupational therapists have a protocol for each of Freud's stages of psychodynamic development, except latency, which is where we just stand by and watch nothing happen. We have the oral phase of spitting and gagging and slurping pudding. We have the anal phase of evacuation and learning to tolerate Play-Doh and wiping with a clean swipe. We have the phallic stage and the banana donning treatment plan. We even have the sensory reduction for the genital stage, and now we add something for the imaginary *naral* phase of development . . . the SNOT protocol.

Recipe for edible SNOT and BOOGERS

BOOGERS

**3 cups granola (best with raisins or other dried fruit for maximum gross out factor)

¼ cup honey

½ cup peanut butter

Mix well with hands (or a large spoon if you must).

Mold into small balls and chill.

When you serve the "boogers," place 2–3 on a small plate and cover with a generous drizzle of edible SNOT.*

SNOT

One 3-ounce package of lime Jello. Make according to directions, but increase hot water by 1 cup. Allow to cool and gel in the fridge (the Jello will be runny but thickened).

Additions to make boogers more "appealing":

fruit by the foot, red, cut into tiny slivers

nuts, chopped

powdered milk

your imagination

* You may have to change the proportions depending on the granola. You want it sticky but dry enough to hold together.

On this day

And from this day forward

THE LIGHTHEARTED PROJECT

Acting on behalf of Families Everywhere

Hereby grants you the right to forever more live

Sensationally

Made in the USA
San Bernardino, CA
19 September 2015